Legacy Of
The Swamp Rat

Tennessee Quarterbacks
Who Just Said No To Alabama

By Chris Cawood

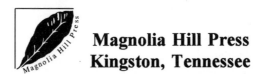

Magnolia Hill Press
Kingston, Tennessee

Copyright © 1994 By Chris Cawood and Magnolia Hill Press, Kingston, Tennessee. All rights reserved.

Cover design by Usha Rao, Graphic Design, Knoxville, Tennessee.

Printed by Berryville Graphics, Berryville, Virginia, United States of America.

Library of Congress Catalog Card Number: 94-076938

ISBN 0-9642231-6-3

5 4 3 2 1

Bobby Scott

Phil Fulmer

Bill Battle

Charles Fulton

Bobby Wyche

Heath #21

Shuler

Daryl Dickey

Warren

Doug Dickey

Dewey "Swamp Rat"

**Best wishes from some of Tennessee's
best quarterbacks and coaches!**

Introduction

If you are one of those who believes that football is just a game, this book is probably not for you. For those of you who *know* that football is socialized war, this is the story of some of the greatest battles of modern football involving two of the South's finest teams–TENNESSEE and ALABAMA.

The one game that has come to mean the most to U-T fans over the decades is the one played on the third Saturday of October. Team success is often measured by this solitary encounter. Coaches come and go, but if they can't beat Alabama, they are not thought of as successful. Ask Bill Battle. He had a great winning percentage–but just one win over Alabama.

Alabama is a measuring stick. The Crimson Tide has long symbolized the top level in success and tradition. Tennessee fans probably take the rivalry more seriously than those from Alabama do now. Alabama has a tough in-state rival in Auburn. But that wasn't always so. From 1907 to 1948, Alabama and Auburn didn't play each other.

Tennessee still doesn't have a strong in-state rival. It only has the little talky-mouth school in Nashville where Commodore faithful have watched the ruin of many a good coach. The black hole of SEC coaching is Vanderbilt. Once a coach goes there, you never hear from him again.

The social calendars of devoted Tennessee fans revolve around the sixteen or so Saturdays between the first of September and the first of January when football is king. People feel better, shop more, laugh louder, and are kinder and gentler when the team is winning and pointing toward the Saturday of destiny when Alabama comes to town or the trip is made to Birmingham for *THE* game.

Not only do Tennessee fans take the Alabama game more seriously, but it is equally true of the national media. *Sports Illustrated* gave the cover to the game in 1967. Now it is usually televised. Word processing terminals have replaced the typewriters and reams of paper formerly used by reporters for the regional and national newspapers for stories leading up to and following the game. A book was written by a non-Tennessean using the *Third Saturday in October* as its title several years ago.

I have to admit my bias. My forefathers were in Tennessee before there was football and before there was the University. I am a Tennessean. I began attending U-T in 1965. And between that time and 1970 when I graduated from Tennessee's College of Law, I watched Charlie Fulton, Dewey Warren, Bubba Wyche, and Bobby Scott quarterback the Volunteers.

This book tells the story of the great victories that Tennessee has had over the rival that epitomizes Southern football. It is bookended by the 7-7 tie in 1965 and the 17-17 draw in 1993. There are eight victories: 1967, 1968, 1969, and 1970; then 1982, 1983, 1984, and 1985. The Tennessee-Alabama series over the past thirty years has been one of streaks. Unfortunately, their streaks have been longer than ours. Things may change.

But this book is more than a recap of the games. Through the eyes and voices of the quarterbacks we are taken back to relive some of those times. Why did they come to Tennessee? What made the Tennessee-Alabama rivalry special in their view? What did they do in these historic games? And what are they doing now? These are some of the questions asked and, I hope, answered in these pages.

These stories of victories are told from the perspective of the **QUARTERBACK**. In these wars, they were the field generals. This is the story of the successful part of the Tennessee-Alabama series since Tennessee switched back to the Slot T and I formations that used a quarterback. When Doug Dickey arrived in late 1963 and prepared his first team for the 1964 season, the single-wing was history.

Some of the real old-timers might ask why the book doesn't include the great game of 1928 with Gene McEver or the ones in the 1930's, 1940's, and 1950's. I have touched on these lightly, but not in as much detail. Each project is limited in scope. This book focuses on the QUARTERBACK and the series since 1965. Certainly, there are great stories of what went before when helmets didn't have the fancy masks, when there was less padding, when you didn't see gloves on players hands or even wraps around their arms. That was a time when players often went both ways, shoes were heavy, cleats were real, and broken noses were expected and worn as badges of courage.

Since 1964, the Tennessee quarterbacks who tied or beat Alabama were a tough gun-slinger type. No one measured up to that description more than the *SWAMP RAT* of the mid 1960's–Dewey Warren. Even an East Tennessee hillbilly can count the quarterbacks on the fingers of both hands and not have to take off his shoes when he numbers the ones who have **JUST SAID NO!** to Alabama. This book is dedicated to these Quarterbacks who led Tennessee to victory or at least stuck their finger in the dike to prevent the flow of the Crimson Tide: **Charlie Fulton, Dewey Warren, Bubba Wyche, Bobby Scott, Alan Cockrell, Tony Robinson, Daryl Dickey, and Heath Shuler.**

MAY THERE BE MANY MORE!

CHRIS CAWOOD

KINGSTON, TENNESSEE–1994

A Brief History of Civilization as We Know It—Tennessee Football 1891-1962

*S*ewanee, not Alabama, was the game of the year in 1891. Played on the Saturday before Thanksgiving in Chattanooga, Tennessee lost in a shutout 0 to 24. That was the first game in Tennessee's organized football history, although the team had played a year earlier as a club sport. Howard A. Ijams was the first U-T quarterback. He played in 1891-93, a hundred years before Heath Shuler.

In reality, it was *The Game of the Year* because it was the only game of the year—a one-game season. The following Saturday, at least six of the Tennessee players joined with others from Knoxville to play visiting Harriman. Harriman won that one 14 to 4, or maybe 8; no one was really sure.

The Knoxville *Journal* was so interested in the area citizens knowing something about the "mysteries of the American game of foot ball" that on the preceding Sunday it had run a large front page story outlining the positions and scoring rules of the new game. The paper encouraged its readers to learn the game and attend, stating that the "street car people have promised good transportation facilities for the day."

The paper quoted an article by "A. A. Stagg of Yale, noted not only for his football work, but equally as well, if not more so, for his baseball work.

"The points which count are: A safety touch down, two points; a touch down, four points; goal, two points," Stagg had written.

1

The quarterback in the young game played a rather different role than he does today. "I place the quarterback in the division with the center, because he is so intimately connected with center work, although in name and position he is counted with the backs. It is his duty to handle every ball which the center rusher rolls back, and he is expected to receive it under all conditions, coming fast or slow, with a bound or not, straight or crooked, for the ball is in play as soon as the center passes it, and he must deliver it to a third person before a gain can be attempted."

The modern fan can readily picture the positions of the quarterback and center and subsequent "roll" of the football in 1891as a modified "shotgun." The quarterback was not allowed to advance the football himself but had to hand it off or "pass" it to a halfback or fullback behind the line of scrimmage.

Stagg described the ideal tackles as "young men built about 5 feet 9 inches in height, weight from 170 to 175 pounds with deep round bodies and heavily muscled, swift runners, quick in movement, hard, sure tacklers." Of course, this size person today would find it hard to make a junior high team.

The inauspicious start in 1891 did not deter the Tennessee team from preparing for the following year when they would play seven games, losing five. Charles Moore, a member of the 1891 team and captain in 1892, is credited with choosing the Orange and White school colors which were later approved by a vote of the student body.

With only 100 or so in attendance at the first game, the team was a long distance from *BIG ORANGE COUNTRY*.

*T*ennessee played out the remainder of the 19th Century without ever encountering Alabama on the gridiron. From 1891 through 1900, the lightly clad team played seven seasons—not fielding teams in 1894, 1895, and 1898. The combined record for those seven seasons was 19 wins, 15 losses, and two ties. Sewanee had beaten them an additional three times for a total cumulative score of 139 for Sewanee and 0 for Tennessee. The team entered the Twentieth Century with the great ignominy of having never defeated Sewanee and looking for a new rival.

They would find one in Alabama. Although Tennessee has played Kentucky and Vanderbilt more times than Alabama, the same feeling of competition is not there as both of those schools' football programs have faded over the last quarter century.

From 1901 through 1914, Tennessee and Alabama met on the football field eleven times. The first one was a six to six draw. Then after Tennessee handled the Alabamans in 1904 by a score of five to zero, Alabama slammed the door on any Tennessee scoring for seven straight games, winning by a total margin of 113 to 0. The first seven games were played in Birmingham.

In 1909, Tennessee first faced their southern tormentors in Knoxville. The series was then interrupted for two years because of the aftermath of the game.

An account of the game put it this way: ". . . (R. W.) Ramsey made about 40 yards through the line but Umpire Elgin called the play back and penalized Tennessee 15 yards for holding. Tennessee protested vigorously.

"Spectators booed Elgin. The crowd followed him to the street car where he was struck on the head with a stone. He was also followed to his hotel where he was subjected to further abuse.

"It should be recorded to the credit of the sportsmen of Knoxville that they did much to protect Elgin and one individual offered a reward of $25 for the name of the umpire's assailant." Alabama won the game 10 to 0.

After not playing for two years, the series was restored to Birmingham in 1912 and to Tuscaloosa in 1913. The 1913, 1928, and 1930 games were the only ones played in Tuscaloosa, with all the others alternating between Knoxville and Birmingham. Except for the war year of 1943, the two have played every year since 1928.

With Alabama having skunked the Tennesseans in 1912 and 1913, the game once again came to Knoxville for 1914. This encounter precipitated another separation of thirteen seasons until 1928.

1914 VOLUNTEERS GO 9 AND 0

Tennessee labored in the depths of mediocrity from 1891 through 1913. Losses to Alabama during that span numbered eight, and, even worse, the team had lost twelve consecutive times to Vanderbilt.

In 1911, Z. G. Clevenger came from Nebraska Wesleyan where he had coached since 1907 to become the first full time football coach for Tennessee. By coincidence, he was playing baseball with the Knoxville team in the Appalachian league when R. C. Matthews asked him to consider the Tennessee coaching job.

Matthews was a professor of mechanical drawing in the Engineering College. But more than that, he was the head cheerleader for the football team on game days. This was the first, and perhaps last, time that the head cheerleader was so instrumental in the hiring of a head coach at Tennessee.

Tennessee was a member of the Southern Intercollegiate Athletic Association at that time. The association had a rule that any school with over 500 male students could not play their freshmen in competition between the schools. Tennessee had between 500 and 600 men enrolled and had to declare its freshmen ineligible.

Coach Clevenger saw this as giving an unfair advantage to such schools as Sewanee—Tennessee's old nemesis—because Sewanee could entice the top players from the prep schools to go to a place like Sewanee where they could play their freshman year.

In a letter written in 1964, Clevenger spoke of those early days at Tennessee: "When I came to Tennessee, there was no spring practice or early fall assembly for footballers. Many of the players participated in either basketball or baseball in addition to football. There was no interference with football. I coached all

4

three sports and was busy the entire nine months of the school year.

"There was nothing attractive about football, and the only players were those with an intense desire to play. We had no money, and there was no such thing as game equipment. The same gear was used for practices and games.

"There was no such thing as a football scholarship, so we had to hold to the boys we had and add to them the best way possible."

Slowly, over the years of 1911, 1912, and 1913, Coach Clevenger, with no paid assistants, built up a strong Tennessee team. The win record increased each year, but he had still not beaten either Vanderbilt or Alabama.

He used the straight T formation and had an excellent quarterback in Knoxvillian Bill May. Clevenger provided a varied mix of runs and passes: "We used mainly the T formation, a special spread and punt formations that are used today. We had all the fundamental plays from this formation, the runs, bucks, split bucks, fake bucks and passes, cross bucks, criss crosses, quarterback sneaks and end runs, quarterback fake and passes, and passes mixed in at all times," he wrote in 1964.

The 1914 season opened with a sense of how good the team was to be with a defeat of Carson-Newman by a score of 89 to 0. There was no hint of any weaknesses in this juggernaut of a team as it rolled over King 55 to 3, Clemson 27 to 0, and Louisville 66 to 0.

In the four games leading up to Alabama week, Tennessee had outscored its opponents 237 to 3. Alabama had also won all three of its games by a combined score of 80 to 0. Two undefeated titans would meet in Knoxville on October 24.

The hard fought struggle in 1913 in Tuscaloosa had set the stage for the theatrics of 1914. On the Alabama campus in 1913, the spectators got completely out of control. Because of the numerous time-outs to clear the injured and boisterous spectators from the field, the last few minutes were played in darkness with only the headlights of automobiles turned onto the field for illumination. Alabama won 6 to 0 to run their string of shutouts over Tennessee to seven.

It may sound like a modern story, but Tennessee in 1914 found out that an Alabama player had already played professional ball—not football but baseball. The athlete's eligibility was questioned. The Southern Association's head ruled that the professional contract made Alabama's star player ineligible for football when the player, Charlie Joplin, declined to sign an affidavit denying that he had played professional baseball.

Tennessee won 17 to 7, but Alabama's coaches, players, and fans went home incensed. The series was halted—not to be resumed until 1928.

This team of 1914 was Tennessee's best to date. They put down Alabama, Chattanooga, Sewanee, and Vanderbilt on consecutive weeks. It was only their second defeat of Alabama. The same was true of Sewanee who had defeated Tennessee in ten of the previous eleven meetings, but was never to defeat them again. It was the first victory over hated Vanderbilt.

The Southern championship belonged to the Volunteers and Z. G. Clevenger with a perfect 9 and 0 record. Clevenger stayed one more year and then went to Kansas State. From Kansas state Tennessee received its next coach in the person of John Bender.

BENDER AND BANKS PRECEDE NEYLAND

With Clevenger going to Kansas State and John Bender coming from Kansas State to Tennessee in 1916, the football program continued on an elevated level. However, the team that was later to become their fiercest rival fell from the schedule.

Bender employed what would today be termed the short punt formation, but stayed with the basics of Clevenger's T. In his first year, the Volunteers posted a 8-0-1 record and again defeated Sewanee and Vanderbilt. World War I interrupted football as Tennessee did not field a team in 1917 or 1918.

Regrouping in 1919, the Volunteers managed a balanced

record of three wins, three losses, and three ties. After getting seven wins against two defeats in 1920, Bender opted to take a position with Knoxville High School rather than stay on as coach at Tennessee. Perhaps part of the reason was that the team once again lost to Vanderbilt, but more importantly, high school football was drawing larger gates than college. This continued to be true for a few more years as is evidenced by U-T's next coach leaving to become the Central High School (of Knoxville) coach after his tenure at Tennessee.

The Southern Intercollegiate Athletic Association saw the last of Tennessee with the ending of the 1920 season and the forming of the Southern Conference for the 1921 season.

M. B. Banks was a graduate of Syracuse and had coached college ball before coming to Tennessee. The first team to play on Shields-Watkins Field was coached by Banks in 1921. Before that they played on Waite Field. Seventeen rows of stands on the west side made the seating capacity 3,200 at the new field.

Banks' teams had fairly good success during his first two years. Tennessee won six games in 1921 and eight in 1922 and first wore orange jerseys under Banks. But he couldn't shake the losing streak to Vanderbilt. In his first three years, Vanderbilt outscored Tennessee 79 to 13 in taking three wins.

When the Volunteers lost five straight in 1924 to close out the season, Banks only had a year left on his contract. The Central High School coaching position began to look more and more alluring. Although Banks managed a winning record of five wins against two defeats in 1925, the process was in motion to bring in someone new. The administration wanted someone who could beat Vanderbilt. An assistant to Banks who had filled in for him during his illness in 1925 looked like an attractive candidate. He was also an Army Captain who was taking charge of the university's ROTC program.

THE NEYLAND ERA:THE SINGLE-WING REPLACES THE T

In 1925, Nathan W. Dougherty was in charge of the athletic program. He is credited with discovering Captain Robert R. Neyland and elevating him to the head coaching position.

Neyland, 33, brought with him two of his former West Point classmates, W. H. Britton and Paul Parker. Neyland was a builder, organizer, and grand strategist. The athletic budget cupboard was almost bare when he took over, but he pushed for expansion of the stands—which would later grow into a stadium under his direction. In 1926, east stands were added to match the west. They accounted for another 3600 seats, bringing the total capacity to 6800.

Beginning in 1926, Neyland installed the powerful single-wing offensive formation and sent the T formation to the scrap heap where it would remain until 1964.

In 1925, Alabama won the Southern Conference championship and the National Championship without playing Tennessee. They repeated the process in 1926. Coach Wallace Wade, who took over in 1923, would eventually lead the Tide to four Southern and three National Championships during his eight years as head coach.

Although they were both in the same conference, Tennessee and Alabama had not played each other since 1914. Neyland wanted to play Alabama—when he thought Tennessee was ready. By 1928, the time had arrived. Neyland had two years of building a team under his belt.

Tennessee had gone eight and one in his initial season. They allowed only 34 points and scored 151. The next year was even better. Tennessee won the Southern Conference championship by outscoring their opponents 245 to 26 while winning eight and tying one. In the same 1927 season, Alabama had slid a bit, ending up with a five-win season against four losses and a tie. The time was right. Neyland sought out Wade to arrange a game.

Coach Wade was so confident Alabama could beat Tennessee, it is told, that he agreed to cut the last two quarters short if the

Tide was too far ahead. He didn't want to embarrass the young Neyland. Neyland just wanted a chance for his "young hillbillies" to play the nationally respected team.

Details were ironed out. Tennessee would have to come to Alabama—and not only to Alabama but to Tuscaloosa—and play at the campus field. This was the same locale of the 1913 game where Tennessee had lost 6 to 0.

Tradition was born through the coincidence of scheduling. The game would be played on October twentieth. **THE THIRD SATURDAY OF OCTOBER.** It would always be so. The third Saturday in October would be reserved for the battle of Southern football supremacy.

Both teams were undefeated. Tennessee had won three going into the game and Alabama two. A common opponent had been Mississippi, which Alabama had shut out 27 to 0. Tennessee bested Mississippi by just one the week before Alabama. Bama was the favorite.

Tennessee's sophomore class included Gene McEver, Bobby Dodd, and Buddy Hackman.

McEver was back to take the opening kickoff. His 98-yard return for a touchdown will always be pointed to as the turning point in the game (although it was the opening play) that put it into the hearts of the young men that they could play with a team of Alabama's caliber. It was the game that established a lasting rivalry and put Tennessee on the national football map.

McEver remembered that run when he talked with Ben Byrd of the Knoxville *Journal* in 1968. "I took it straight up the middle. It wasn't any special thing we had worked on—just the regular kickoff return.

"A lot of people don't remember that Alabama came back to score a touchdown three plays after we had scored. They just took the kickoff and marched right through us, and I remember thinking, 'Uh-oh, this is going to be one of those games where we lead for one minute and that's all.'"

But it wasn't all. McEver caught a pass for another

touchdown. An Alabama punt was blocked out of the end zone for a safety, and Tennessee won 15 to 13.

McEver wasn't through. He never played on a UT team that lost a game. His three years of varsity play (1928, 1929, and 1931) saw Tennessee go 9-0-1 each year. Each of the three years Kentucky tied the Volunteers. McEver didn't play the 1930 season because of a knee injury. His team beat Alabama each year he played. Tennessee lost to Alabama in 1930 when McEver was out.

Frank Thomas succeeded Wade as Alabama's coach in 1931, but he could not beat Tennessee until a lanky end from Fordyce, Arkansas, became a sophomore for the Crimson Tide in 1933. The three years that Paul Bryant played for Alabama were hard ones on Tennessee. Tennessee lost 12 to 6 in 1933, 13 to 6 in 1934, while Alabama was on the way to a National Championship, and worst of all, 25 to 0 in 1935 when the young cub Bear was not supposed to play.

The Alabama end had been reported "definitely lost for the season" but entered the game to catch passes all over the field as the Tide blanked the Vols.

Neyland could not be held responsible for the skunking by Alabama in 1935. He had been called to active duty in the Panama Canal Zone. The coaching duties were turned over to assistant coach W. H. Britton who compiled a four win, five loss season record.

Major Neyland returned in 1936, and the rivalry with Alabama heated up with a scoreless draw. He was again laying the groundwork for an amazing run of three years (1938-40) in which the Volunteers won thirty-one games and lost only two. During those three years, Tennessee outscored its opponents by a combined score of 827 to 75. This ended Neyland's second successful stint with Tennessee as he was once again called up to active duty for World War II.

THE BARNHILL YEARS—1941-1945

Major Neyland was called off to World War II, promoted

10

to colonel, and began to build airports and bridges. While his mind and body were occupied with the war efforts, the Tennessee coaching job was turned over to John Barnhill, a former Neyland pupil.

Barnhill was a native Tennessean from Savannah. While his record at Tennessee was very good overall, his Volunteers lost three times to Alabama and managed a tie with the Crimson Tide in their fourth encounter.

There was no team in 1943 because of the war, and that was where the even and odd years switched in the schedule of the Tennessee-Alabama third Saturday in October clash. Since 1928, the teams had played in even years at Alabama and in odd-numbered years at Tennessee. Tennessee got the game in 1944 and has played Alabama at Knoxville in every even-numbered year since.

Under Barnhill, the Volunteers went to the Rose Bowl after the 1944 season and lost to Southern California 25 to 0 on January 1, 1945. Two years earlier, Tennessee beat Tulsa 14 to 7 in the Sugar Bowl.

Barnhill proved himself an able coach, but he and every one else knew the job was once again to be Neyland's when he returned from war duty.

On May 7, 1945, an event occurred in Valdosta, Georgia, that was little noticed by anyone except for the Warren family. Dewey Madison Warren was born to Hazel and Dewey Warren. Soon they would move to Savannah, Georgia.

When Neyland returned as a general, Barnhill turned the reins back over to the coach and shortly after went to Arkansas to coach. In 1949, he became athletic director. In that position, he hired such notables as Bowden Wyatt and, later, Frank Broyles as head coaches.

NEYLAND RELOADS FOR A NATIONAL CHAMPIONSHIP

It seemed that every time Robert Neyland returned to U-T from military assignments he came back not only with a higher

11

rank but with a desire and ability to take Tennessee to another level of football accomplishment. It was never easy. The records in 1947 and 1948 were two of the worst ever in Neyland history. The team only broke even in wins, losses, and ties.

But the foundation was being laid, the blocks being placed in the trenches, and out of it would rise a national championship team—the only one in the Neyland era—in 1951. In 1949, Neyland was able to squeeze seven wins from his war-starved ranks of Volunteers. Neyland tied his winning record of 1938 in 1950 when the Volunteers won eleven, losing a squeaker to Mississippi State in the second game of the season. Tennessee was ranked Number 1 by the Dunkel poll but not by the ones that really counted.

Finally, in 1951, General Neyland gained the goal aspired to by every coach and player. The Volunteers ran through an undefeated regular season, outscoring opponents 373 to 88.

The Vols beat Alabama in their first televised game 27 to 13. The season was slightly marred by a loss to Maryland in the Sugar Bowl. However, the glory was in hand before the gloomy day in New Orleans. The Vols were consensus National Champions.

In just over a year from the winning of the National Championship, General Neyland's health declined to a point that he had to step aside as coach. His trusted aide, Harvey Robinson, took over, but the team just was never the same. The record slid to four losses in 1953 and six the following year.

It was impossible to follow a legend.

"I never wanted to be head coach," Robinson said in an interview with a Knoxville *Journal* reporter in 1964.

"He was a master in organization, recruiting of players, and obtaining the full measure of a player's ability," Robinson, a North Carolina native, observed.

"General Neyland was the greatest coach in the history of American football."

The U-T administration and Volunteer fans yearned for the

return of a native Tennessean who had played under Neyland to restore the glory years. They turned to a coach at Arkansas.

Bowden Wyatt played his high school ball at Roane County High in nearby Kingston. He was a handsome man with a prominent jaw, dark hair, and dimples. He could have been a movie star.

In his second season, Wyatt was named SEC Coach of the Year after the Volunteers won the championship behind the running and passing of Heisman runnerup Johnny Majors.

In 1957, the record slipped to seven wins, but the Vols went to the Gator Bowl and beat Bear Bryant's Texas A&M team. Bryant moved to Alabama in 1958, but the Vols prevailed 14 to 7.

Tennessee began slipping in 1959. The Vols tied the Crimson tide with seven each, but lost the last three games of the season to Mississippi, Kentucky, and Vanderbilt by an embarrassing total score of 7 to 71. This was immediately following a monumental victory over LSU and All-American Billy Cannon in Knoxville by a 14 to 13 score on a goal-line stop that is discussed on occasion to this day at Hoo-Ray's in Knoxville.

All the distractions of Neyland's illness and his duties as acting athletic director weighed heavily on the loyal Wyatt. When others wanted to get rid of Neyland as athletic director, he defended him.

"There are some who would like the General to stay away from the practice field. He will have a seat in the middle of the field any time he desires. If he needs help, I'll escort him to that seat.

"If he gets weak and wants to crawl, I'll get down and crawl with him.

"Bob Neyland loves this school. More than anyone else, he has made it into one of the biggest and best in the South.

"He's done too much for too many for anyone ever to deny him the right of doing as he wishes here at Tennessee."

Neyland was hospitalized in New Orleans in late 1961 and died early in 1962. His imprint on Tennessee football stands as a memorial to his genius and vigor.

Which was his best team? Could it have been the National Champion team of 1951? Or 1938? Was it the 1939 team that was unscored on? This was the same team that last beat Sewanee. The team that had been the thorn in the side of Tennessee when football was new and young has not appeared on its schedule since.

On **The third Saturday in October** in 1962, before Tennessee played Alabama, the stadium surrounding Shields-Watkins field was named in honor of the coach who had built it—block by block and team by team. From a stadium with a seating capacity of 6,800 in his first year, General Robert R. Neyland had watched it grow into one that could hold 52,227 when Alabama came to town.

On the visiting sideline was another coach who was destined to be a legend. He never beat Neyland while he coached at Kentucky. Now in his fifth year at Alabama, Paul (Bear) Bryant was going for his second win against Tennessee while at Alabama. He had won a National Championship the year before. He had a sophomore quarterback that he had high hopes for by the name of Joe Willie Namath. What followed were to be the years of the quarterbacks.

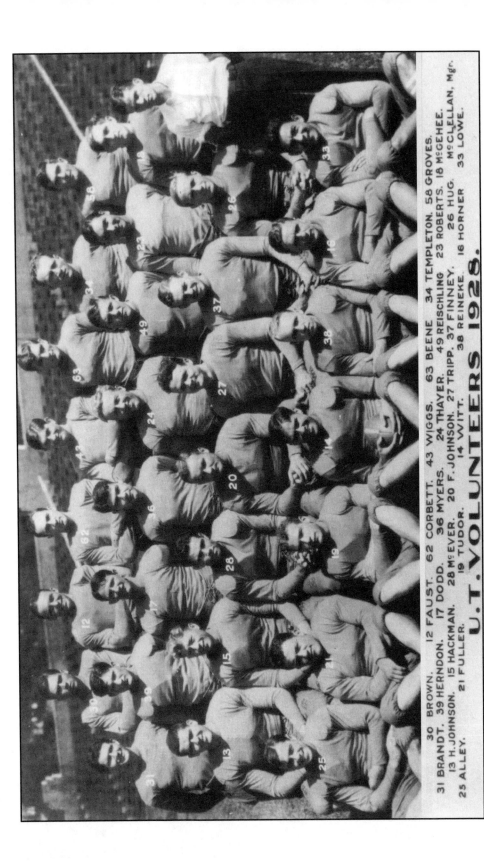

30 BROWN. 12 FAUST. 62 CORBETT. 43 WIGGS. 63 BEENE. 34 TEMPLETON. 58 GROVES.
31 BRANDT. 39 HERNDON. 17 DODD. 36 MYERS. 24 THAYER. 49 REISCHLING 23 ROBERTS. 18 McGEHEE.
13 H.JOHNSON. 15 HACKMAN. 28 McEVER. 20 F.JOHNSON. 27 TRIPP. 37 FINNEY. 26 HUG. McCLELLAN, Mgr.
25 ALLEY. 21 FULLER. 19 TUDOR. 14 WITT. 38 REINEKE. 16 HORNER 33 LOWE.

U. T. VOLUNTEERS 1928.

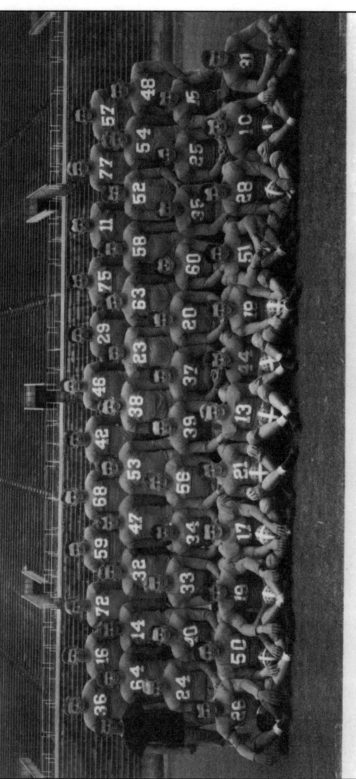

1938 VOLS
UNIVERSITY OF TENNESSEE

Front Row: 26-Ott,50-Sellers,19-Andridge,17-Bartholomew,21-Warren,13-Barnes,44-Bailey,18-Webber,51-Steiner,28-Bacon,10-Montgomery,31-Coleman.

Second Row: 24-Hendricks,40-Eldred,33-Cowan,34-McCarren,56-Woodruff,39-Hunter,37-Capt.Wyatt,20-Little,60-Herring,35-Sneed,25-Wood,15-Duncan, .

Third Row: Mgr.Prater,64-Rike,14-Thompson,32-Mallen,47-Cifers,53-Clay,38-Melton,23-Tenner,63-Ackerman,58-Luttrell,52-West,54-Shires,48-Lampley.

Top Row: 36-Molignti,16-Broome,72-Carego,59-Sexton,68-Hubbuck,42-Suffridge,46-Whitehead,29-Spirakle,75-Smith,11-Coffman,77-Foxx,57-Thomas.

33. NOEL 52-WEST 10-DISSWAYNE 63-ACKERMAN 50-EDMISTON 54-SHIRES 39-CANNON 65-CLARKE 62-BALITSARIS 55-GRAVES 66-HUNT 27-VICK 46-POWERS 12-BRYSON
ELDRIDGE 42-SUFFRIDGE 31-COLEMAN 15-ABRELIA 56-BROWN 45-WHITEHEAD 60-CANTRELL 58-LUTTRELL 48-JOHNSON 41-SYPHERS 14-THOMPSON 19-ANDRIDGE 35-MORRIS 20-NEWMAN 61-TUCKER
23-TANNER 36-MOLINSKI 47-CIFERS 72-CAFEGO 57-THOMAS 53-CLAY 11-COFFMAN 17-BARTHOLOMEW 64-RIKE 32-WALLEN 68-HUBBUCK 13-BARNES 75-SMITH 40-HUBBELL
26-O'NEIL 22-BUTLER 28-BACON 29-FOSTER 44-BALES 18-WEBER 51-STEINER 77-FOXX 34-PEEL 30-FORD 33-MULLEY 21-WARREN

"VOLS" 1939

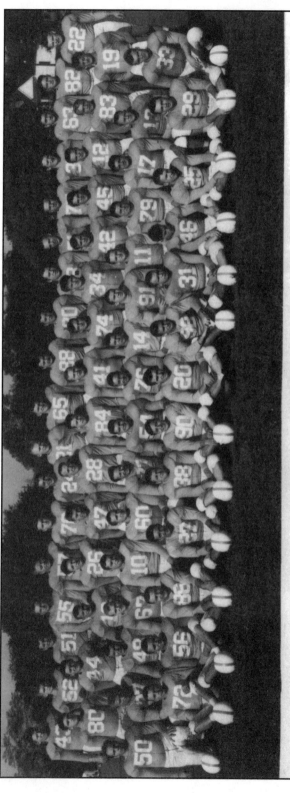

1951 VOLS

FRONT ROW - 72 Hahn, 56 Haslam, 86 Kozar, 27 Lauricella, 38 Michels, 90 Bob Davis, 20 Rechichar, 92 Lyons, 31 Stokes, 46 John Davis, 25 Kesets, 29 Watson, 33 Byrd.

SECOND ROW - 50 Addonizio, 37 Bordinger, 48 Butler, 67 Daffer, 10 Polofsky, 60 Pearman, 77 Payne, 54 Holohan, 76 Jasper, 14 Martin, 91 Atkins, 11 Blackstock, 79 Rotroff, 17 Maiure, 13 Shires.

THIRD ROW - 80 Coloninger, 44 Romeo, 16 Campbell, 26 Alexander, 47 Ernsberger, 28 Sekanovich, 84 Laughlin, 41 Vest, 74 Munro, 34 Herrmann, 42 Meyer, 45 Morgan, 12 Bill Fulton, 83 Stokely Fulton, 19 Hubbard.

TOP ROW - 43 Fisher, 52 Crowson, 51 Patterson, 55 Trubits, 57 Myers, 70 Twitty, 24 Hyde, 21 Franklin, 65 Boring, 88 Stowers, 30 Keller, 18 Barbish, 71 Powell, 75 Moeller, 35 Lis, 63 Neyland, 82 Williams, 22 Jumper.

The Bear Visits the Swamp Rat

The coach leaned against the fence, flipped the cigarette butt to the ground, and crushed out any fire left in it with the sole of his brown leather shoe. He squinted toward the middle of the field where the high schoolers were scrimmaging.

Why was he here? The only off-week of the 1962 season and he had traveled from Tuscaloosa to Savannah, Georgia. The late afternoon sun was low on the western horizon, striking him directly in the face. He should walk around to the other side where there was a clump of parents and assistant high school coaches gathered. But then he would have to answer their questions: Why was he here? And who was he looking at?

Having won the National Championship in 1961, Paul "Bear" Bryant was a marked man wherever he went. Word was bound to get out. "The Bear was down here looking at a local boy. Better send your coach." Then all the other Southeastern Conference schools would send their people into town.

He needed to get away from Tuscaloosa. The week before, Georgia Tech had beaten his Alabama team by a point to ruin a perfect season. The following week they had to play Auburn.

He wasn't sure what he was seeing in this kid that Jenkins High School coach Lamar Leachman had touted so highly. He should be used to it by now—the puffing up of every high school kid with a little talent into a sure bet All-American.

He brought the crumpled piece of paper out of his coat

19

pocket and looked at the note. "Great arm. Tough. Hard-nosed. A winner. Dewey Warren. Swamp Rat." He put it back. He had been watching him all practice, and he was still not sure he was seeing a player that Alabama needed.

On the other side of the field, he joined Coach Leachman for a little gruff-whispered chat.

"Coach Bryant, what do you think of him?"

The Bear shook his head slowly, not looking at Leachman, but staring into the backfield where Warren was setting up for a pass. "I'll have to send someone back for a game, Coach. It's hard to tell much at a practice."

"He's a good one, Coach Bryant. You ought to save a scholarship for him."

Bryant lit another cigarette and cupped his hand to shelter it from the wind that was now picking up. "Why hasn't Coach Butts signed him? Butts tries to get all the good Georgia boys. We talk a lot on the phone, you know."

Leachman shook his head, turned, and spit toward the ground. "I don't know. Someone said he didn't think Warren could play college ball. But I know he can."

Bryant barely nodded. "So, Butts doesn't want him?"

Leachman shook his head. "He's missing a good one."

"What about Tennessee? You played there. Are they after him?"

"I talked to Bob Woodruff. He has some kin down here. But, you see, Coach Bryant, Tennessee is still single-wing. There's some talk there might be a change to the T. But if they stay single-wing, the Swamp Rat would never fit in. He's a thrower. He's not all that much on running, although he's a good runner for high school.

"They're looking for a tailback like Majors or Lauricella. I was there with both of them. Dewey's not like that, but he'd fit into a passing setup like yours real well."

"Maybe. I thought you said he was a linebacker too. Couldn't he play linebacker for Tennessee?"

"He's tough enough. But I think he's a quarterback with a linebacker's nerve and aggressiveness."

"Tennessee could use some linebackers. Any school that would let a bunch of poor little skinny kids like ours score thirty-four points on them last year and twenty-seven this year could use some linebackers." Bryant turned and looked the Tennessee alumnus in the eye. There was no hint of a grin.

"You ought to take him, Coach Bryant. Or else, he may end up being on a team that beats you."

Bryant nodded. "Yeah, that's possible. But I've just got so much room. Quarterback is not a real high priority with me now. That kid I got from up in Pennsylvania—Namath—is just a sophomore. He may turn out alright if I can just calm him down.

"Then I got that Sloan boy we picked up from within spitting distance of Knoxville. He may turn out okay, too. Then there's supposed to be a good kid down in Foley, Alabama, who could play some quarterback if he doesn't get killed first. He looks as fragile as a matchstick to me. Stabler's his name."

"You don't think you could use another quarterback?"

"I'm not saying for sure, Coach Leachman. But if you have any connections at Tennessee and you want to see that boy play in college, you might think about sending him there."

Coach Bryant and Coach Leachman both looked back toward the field where Warren had just tackled a defensive back who had intercepted a pass.

"Linebacker, Leachman. Linebacker."

Bear Bryant went back to Tuscaloosa, beat Auburn the following week 38 to 0, and then finished with a 17 to 0 victory over Oklahoma in the Orange Bowl. He never made any further contact to recruit Dewey Warren.

Wally Butts of Georgia passed on Warren too.

Coach Lamar Leachman who played at Tennessee in 1952, 1953, and 1955, was able to interest Bob Woodruff in Warren. U-T gambled and took him. If they didn't go to the T formation, he would at least get a shot at linebacker.

In 1963, Dewey "Swamp Rat" Warren reported to Tennessee to play for "interim" head coach Jim McDonald who coached under "interim" athletic director Bob Woodruff. Warren quarterbacked the scout team and even played some linebacker as a freshman in practice to further steel his toughness.

On November 16, 1963, the Jim McDonald-coached Volunteers lost their fifth game of the season to Mississippi. There were two games remaining, but the word was out that McDonald was through. There would be a new coach the next year. The single-wing would be out and the T formation would return for the first time in 38 years.

Six days after the Mississippi loss, President John F. Kennedy was assassinated in Dallas. Football was just a game, but life was real.

Doug Dickey to Tennessee

Most everyone who was alive in 1963 during those tragic three days in Dallas remembers where they were when they heard the news that President Kennedy had been shot. Doug Dickey doesn't remember.

It probably says more for the pressure that a young offensive coordinator, who was also being considered for the head coaching job at Tennessee, was under at the time than for a lack of memory. Doug Dickey's memory is otherwise excellent. Over thirty years after the fact, he can recall detail after detail of his arriving at Tennessee and rattle off players' names from his first team of Volunteers.

Son of a college professor, he learned early the vagabond life of college instructors, administrators, and coaches who follow the fortunes of opportunity from state to state. Born in South Dakota, he moved with his father and mother to follow a job opening for his father, Dallas, at Louisiana State University in Baton Rouge. Doug was then three.

At fourteen, Doug loaded up and moved again to another Southeastern Conference school—Florida. All this and his father wasn't even a coach. There the young Douglas Adair Dickey took root as a ninth grader and was able to display his athletic ability.

It was only natural that the Florida football coach, Bob Woodruff, who had played on that great Neyland team of 1938, should notice the lanky quarterback and entice him to stay at home. In the early fifties, Dickey was the quarterback for the Florida Gators.

"Doug was one of the most intelligent quarterbacks I ever saw. He took over when Haywood Sullivan left us for a baseball bonus and led our team to the Gator Bowl in 1952," Woodruff was later to say about his quarterback.

Out of college, he coached for a year at a high school in St. Petersburg before joining the Army. Dickey describes his longevity in the Army in football terms.

"I was in the service for three football seasons. The last one I coached a team at Fort Carson. When I got out of the service in the spring of 1958, I went to the University of Arkansas. I was there for six years with Frank Broyles." John Barnhill, a former Tennessee coach, was Arkansas' athletic director. In 1961, Dickey's college coach, Woodruff, returned to Tennessee as an assistant coach.

While Jim McDonald was trying his best to salvage the 1963 season, there were rumblings across the state for change. "Throw out the single-wing and go to the T formation. Bring in a young coach who knows the T formation and how to coach quarterbacks."

McDonald had come in as coach under very trying circumstances. He had come to Tennessee to help Bowden Wyatt get the Vols back onto the winning track. He was goal oriented. "Set a goal and work until you achieve it and then pick another goal," was his way of putting it. A series of things happened to make it impossible for McDonald to continue as head coach.

Neyland died in early 1962. Wyatt's days as coach were numbered. Woodruff moved up to interim athletic director. McDonald wasn't finally selected until June of 1963 to be head coach. He had only three weeks before meeting his first squad and not very long until the first game in September.

His Vols beat the lesser teams on the schedule like Richmond, Chattanooga, Tulane, Kentucky, and Vanderbilt. But they were no match for the real SEC teams, losing to Auburn, Mississippi State, and then a shutout on the third Saturday in October to Alabama. The Crimson Tide had rolled 35 to 0. Tennessee's fans and supporters could take it no longer. They wanted to be competitive. There were only 21,696 fans at the last game with Vanderbilt. Not only were the Vols not winning consistently, but small crowds meant lost revenue. Money talked.

Neyland was dead. Long live his successor.

The single-wing was dead. Long live the T and its variations. "Give us a quarterback," was heard from Mountain City to Memphis.

An Arkansas newspaper writer described Dickey in 1963, as a man who *HAD* to be coach.

Toward the end of the 1963 season, Bob Woodruff called up his old quarterback.

Dickey described it this way in 1994: "Coach Woodruff said he would like to recommend me for head coach. He was going to put a package together. He would be the athletic director, and I would be the head coach. He was going to propose that to the president of U-T.

"He said if I was interested, I needed to visit a couple of people. One was Colonel Tom Elam and the other was the president of U-T, Andy Holt. Once I visited with the president, he agreed, and within a couple of hours, I was the football coach."

Some speculated that if McDonald had thumped Vanderbilt by a larger margin than fourteen, he would have saved his job. Not likely. The wheels were already in motion. Dickey said it was "somewhere late in the season" when Woodruff contacted him.

It moved swiftly after the last game. On Sunday McDonald was notified. By Monday, it was known that Dickey was the new coach and it was in all the newspapers.

Dickey assumed the coaching duties at thirty-one years of age. It has now been thirty-one years since he became Tennessee's head coach in December of 1963.

How did he and others describe this young, former quarter-

25

back, former offensive coordinator, and now new head coach? "We have found the young coach we need," athletic board members said.

Frank Broyles said, "Doug is the man I would recommend to succeed me. I don't know of any other young coach who has better qualifications."

Dickey himself said, "I can't remember a time when I didn't plan a future in football. As a high school player, I wanted either to be a pro player or a coach. After I played at Florida, a coaching opportunity opened up and I grabbed it." His only goal was "to have a better football team each year until Tennessee is back where it belongs."

Dickey stood six feet two and a half inches when he came to Tennessee and weighed two hundred pounds. He was described as an inexhaustible worker who often visited eight high schools in a day recruiting. He brought with him a wife, JoAnne, and four sons, Donald, Daniel, David, and two-year-old Daryl.

Dickey hit the ground running. He started recruiting with former coach and then assistant athletic director Jim McDonald. By mid-December, he and McDonald had visited three or four key prospects. "I've always thought it was a very, very noble thing on Jim's part to do that. He was very much a team player. And I always appreciated very much what he did."

On January 22, 1964, an event occurred in Tallahassee, Florida, which would later have an effect on the Dickey family, and especially two-year-old Daryl. A son, Kevin Altoona, was born to Johnny and Jean Robinson.

Less than two months from the time that Dickey arrived, tragedy struck the athletic family. Assistant basketball coach Bill Gibbs was killed in a plane crash at Gainesville, Florida, on February 3, 1964. No one knew then that would be just the first of three that would follow in successive years.

Gibbs' death was a blow to the whole athletic community, but especially to basketball head coach Ray Mears. The coaching staff pulled together and went on with its business.

26

At the time, Mears' basketball teams were reaping unusual support from a predominant football following. Danny Schultz, A. W. Davis, Sid Elliott, Bobby Hogsett, and others were lighting up Big Orange Country.

Mears was a promoter. He coined the term "Big Orange Country" and gladly turned it over to the university for use. In March 1994, he was asked if he had thought about registering the term and making any money from it. "It didn't cross my mind at the time. I see now where others in different parts of the country have done that with other phrases. I was just trying to build support."

At first, Big Orange applied almost exclusively to the basketball team. It did not take root with the football side of athletics for a couple of years. And there was good reason for it. There was suspicion that the players Dickey inherited were not big enough, tough enough, or fast enough to compete in the Southeastern Conference.

The Knoxville *Journal*'s Ed Harris had written on the day after Dickey's selection: "The number one problem facing Dickey will be to find a T-formation quarterback for next season."

Dickey responded, "With the exception of quarterback, there is no great transition from the present system to the T."

Dewey "Swamp Rat" Warren had labored through the 1963 season on the freshman team. He played some quarterback on the scout teams and occasionally crossed the line of scrimmage to take out any frustrations he might have built up at the linebacker's position. He was, obviously, delighted with the change to the T formation.

If new coach Dickey was looking for quarterbacks in his new recruits, a couple of the ones signed out of that high school class were doubtful in that regard. Dickey honored all commitments previously made and tried to pick up new prospects. There were at least two future quarterbacks that signed with Tennessee within a couple of months.

The best all-round football player in Tennessee high schools that year was probably Charlie Fulton of Memphis Whitehaven. He led his school to the number one ranking in Tennessee and an undefeated season. That was before playoffs when ranking was decided by polls—sort of like the highest classification of college football these days.

Dickey knew about Fulton before he became Tennessee's head coach. Being at Arkansas, Dickey had kept up with the Memphis standout.

"Did you recruit Fulton as a quarterback or as an athlete?" Dickey was asked in 1994.

"As a quarterback," he answered unhesitatingly.

The problem was that Memphis Whitehaven was a single-wing school. Charlie Fulton was a tailback. He had never taken a snap from center.

Perhaps another quarterback recruit of that year was an even more unlikely candidate to succeed at Tennessee. Joseph Murry Wyche Jr., affectionately named "Bubba" by his older brother, did not play football in high school as a senior. He had done very well as a sophomore and junior but not as a senior.

In practice, before the start of the 1963 high school season, the highly regarded athlete from downtown Atlanta had a serious injury to his left knee that required surgery to the anterior cruciate ligament. Practically all the schools that had been recruiting him backed off. The injury could be career ending.

Tennessee offered him a one year scholarship. He accepted the offer and vowed to himself to make the best of it.

So, Dickey ended the recruiting season with a tailback he hoped to make into a quarterback and a quarterback with a repaired knee who might not ever be able to withstand the rigors of college football. In all, seven high school quarterbacks were signed.

"Two things are needed for football success," Dickey told a reporter in late December of 1963. "Ability and effort. At times a team with lesser ability but with more desire will win."

That had to be his program for 1964. None of his recruits would be eligible to play as freshmen even if they could have

28

helped. Practice opened with seventy-one prospects on September 1, 1964, in preparation for the opening game with Chattanooga on September 19. The coaching staff was composed of Bill Anderson, Vince Gibson, Charles Rash, Bill Majors, Chuck Rohe, George McKinney, Charlie Coffey, Jimmy Dunn, Jack Kile, George Cafego, and trainer Mickey O'Brien.

On the first day of September, the Swamp Rat was listed as one of the sophomores contending for the starting quarterback position. Within ten days, it was decided to redshirt him.

Dickey's "quarterback problem" was amply illustrated by a photo in the September 10 edition of the Knoxville *Journal*. Shown behind center Frank Emanuel in a semi-circle ready to receive the snap were four prospects "battling it out for the starting quarterback position." They were David Leake, Art Galiffa, Johnny Covington, and Hal Wantland.

Dickey was not being cute. The quarterback position was still up for grabs with only nine days until the opening game. Wantland, Galiffa, and Leake all got their chances during the year.

The team was young throughout. A pair of sophomores—Harold Stancell and Jerry Smith—would open as defensive backs.

A crowd of 25,000 was expected for the opener with Chattanooga. Several thousand of those would be young musicians from more than forty high schools who were there for a marching contest.

Dickey did an outstanding job of getting the "effort" he talked about out of his young team. The start wasn't all that auspicious with a 10 to 6 win over the Mocs. But the next week heads were turned when the young Vols held Auburn to three points but were unable to score any of their own.

A day after the Auburn game, the Warren Commission issued its report and finding that "Lee Harvey Oswald—and Lee Harvey Oswald alone—murdered John F. Kennedy." It's doubtful that Dickey had time to read the full report with Mississippi State, Boston College, and Alabama staring him in the face over the next

29

three weeks.

The new Dickey look of the Volunteers got more attention when they knocked off the next two opponents to take a three win, one loss record into the third Saturday of October. However, Alabama was undefeated, having allowed a total of nine points in its first four games and averaging twenty-eight points itself. Joe Willie Namath was out of Bryant's doghouse and the senior quarterback. He didn't lack nerve or brilliance. In their last three meetings with Tennessee, Bryant's boys had outscored the Volunteers 96 to 10.

Enthusiasm swelled as 48,500 spectators filled the stands. Could Tennessee's surge and youthful enthusiasm stem the Tide? Would Dickey turn it around his first year? Was the magic back? Could the Bear be sent back down the river in a boat instead of walking on water?

No. Alabama 19, Tennessee 8.

"I think this game will help us in the long run," Dickey said.

And it was true. In the second half, the Volunteers outscored Alabama eight to three. Confidence was building. The Vols had scored the most points on the Crimson Tide of any team so far in the season and had held them to the least. Only two teams would hold Alabama to fewer points and only three would score more points on the Crimson Tide during the remainder of the season than Tennessee had.

Alabama went on to an undefeated regular season and another National Championship.

Dickey's first Tennessee team finished with four wins, five losses, and a tie. However, the Vols had beaten two SEC schools and tied another. Depth and some skill were still missing. Dickey would recruit depth and have a skilled player at quarterback in 1965.

Youthful coach.

Doug Dickey

1994 Athletic Director

Coach Doug Dickey with two quarterbacks who gave Tennessee four wins over Alabama

1965-Charlie Fulton

With a large atlas laid out before him, Charlie Fulton, as a highly sought senior in high school, could study the locations of all the cities of schools of the Southeastern Conference. Practically all of them wanted him. And there were others too.

About four hundred miles due south was Baton Rouge and Louisiana State University. That's where he wanted to go. He could wear the purple and gold and be a flashy Tiger.

Due east about the same distance was the University of Tennessee, the preference of his father. The University of Mississippi at Oxford was the nearest. They had beaten U-T five straight years, which was practically a lifetime to a young man who would only be seventeen when he graduated from Shelby County's Whitehaven High School.

A gifted athlete who worked hard at reaching his potential both physically and mentally, Charles Beauford Fulton could have chosen any of the schools he located on the map. They all wanted the elusive runner who could pass. He had just led his football team to the mythical state championship decided by a poll of sportswriters.

His athletic ability was not limited to the grass field with stripes every five yards. He excelled as a guard on the basketball team. The year before he had pitched two no-hitters for the baseball team. In his spare time he ran track. On Sunday he sang hymns at his church and also performed vocally for the high school

33

chorus. His grades were so good, and would remain so good, that he would eventually make Academic All-SEC for two of his college seasons.

It was no wonder that this well-rounded youth was sought by many. There was only one small drawback. Whitehaven was one of the few high schools that still ran the single-wing made famous by Neyland and Tennessee. Now Tennessee was switching to the T formation under first-year coach Doug Dickey. Fulton had never taken a snap from center.

But that didn't matter to Dickey. He saw the talent in the young Fulton. He had heard of it while still a coach at Arkansas.

There was competition for Fulton. He visited Alabama and came away very impressed with the facilities. But it just wasn't for him. He narrowed his list down to LSU, Memphis State, and Tennessee, with perhaps some thought to Mississippi.

Tennessee was a long drive away; the interstates weren't finished. But his dad preferred U-T. Charlie respected his father, Tennessee did have a fine tradition, and Harvey Robinson still wanted him. Robinson was the backfield coach in 1963 under Jim McDonald. When Dickey came in, George McKinney took over the recruiting of Fulton and concluded the deal. Robinson had recruited the talented tailback for two years, and his efforts paid off.

Dickey saw Fulton as a type of quarterback he wanted. "We recruited him to be our quarterback because we knew the option play was a very high part of our offense. In those days, options, bootlegs, and a running style quarterback was what we needed. The sprint-out passes and a running quarterback was going to be our style. Charlie Fulton was the epitome of that in those days."

He wasn't real big—about 5' 10" and 175 pounds. He was angular and elusive, as hard to catch as a young steer in a barn lot. You either had to have a rope or enough people to surround him to bring him down. A raw-boned, dark-complected youth who could shave in the shower in the morning and still need another one before breakfast was over, he would fit right into the Tennessee tradition of great tailbacks—and perhaps a new tradition of quarterback.

In 1994, Doug Dickey said, "Charlie Fulton could probably have saved the single-wing for Tennessee. Charlie was the premier player in the state of Tennessee as far as a skill position player is concerned. He would have been a great tailback for Tennessee. He would have been a Hank Lauricella type without a doubt in my mind."

Fulton came to Tennessee for fall practice and joined six other quarterback hopefuls on the freshman team. It soon narrowed down to him and Bubba Wyche as the promising duo who were getting more snaps in practice.

They each had strengths and weaknesses. Wyche's left knee was still not back to the way it was before surgery a year before. He could pass, but he wasn't as mobile running. Fulton had no trouble running if he didn't drop the ball on the exchange from center. "It took me quite a while just to be able to get the snap from center," Fulton would later say.

Freshmen were ineligible for varsity competition anyway, so they both had time to learn and get well.

George McKinney coached the freshmen during their games in 1964. They lost three out of four, with losses to Georgia Tech, Vanderbilt, and Kentucky. Their lone win was over Virginia Tech in the last game of their short season. Both Fulton and Wyche played at quarterback in the games, and both did reasonably well under the circumstances. This was the first year for the T formation at U-T, there was a new coaching staff, and the varsity wasn't doing much better.

Most of the time the freshmen joined with those being redshirted to form the scout team for the varsity to beat up on. "Redshirting" is the procedure by which a player is held out of varsity competition for a year and still allowed the extra year to play. In 1964, a player was eligible for three varsity participation seasons plus a freshman year. The "scout team" was the group of freshmen, redshirts, and second or third team players who would try to mimic what the varsity's next opponent would employ on offense and defense.

After a couple of weeks of fall practice, Fulton and Wyche had another future quarterback join them on the scout team. The coaching staff decided they had enough varsity quarterback prospects with whom to be concerned without wasting a year of Dewey "Swamp Rat" Warren's eligibility.

The scout team only had use for so many quarterbacks, so when he wasn't needed there, Warren would often go over to the defensive side and bang heads as a linebacker. When it came Alabama week, none of the three was able to imitate the skill of Joe Namath to the degree that U-T's varsity needed. Of course, no one in the country could have.

Warren remembers watching that game as a redshirt from the sidelines. "Joe Namath came up here and beat us on one leg. He wasn't well. It was great to watch someone of his talent."

Freshmen didn't dress for the varsity games, so Fulton and Wyche didn't get a very close view of the All-American quarter-back performing on Shields-Watkins field.

The 1964 campaign ended with Warren, Fulton, and Wyche all knowing they would be in the hunt for the starting quarterback position in 1965. It was competitive. Warren had been there a year longer than the other two. Fulton was a better runner and option player than the other two. Wyche was as determined as anyone to make something good happen if he was given the opportunity.

Fulton knew that his weaknesses were in the center exchange and familiarity with the varsity receivers. In the late spring and early summer of 1965 he remedied that. Instead of going home to Memphis when school was out after the spring quarter, he joined center Bob Johnson and end-receiver Johnny Mills at a camp for youthful footballers at Tellico. They worked as counselors for the youth during the hours of the camp, but when they had their own time, they spent it on snaps between Johnson and Fulton and passes from Fulton to Mills.

They had nothing else to do. "I mean it was in the middle of nowhere," Fulton later explained. Thousands of repetitions later he came into fall practice as the one to beat for the quarterback job.

Wyche had been shifted to play some defensive back during spring practice but once again injured his left knee. Surgery was delayed during the spring and summer with hopes that the knee would rehabilitate without it. It didn't. Bubba would face the surgeon's knife again in the fall. He was lost for the 1965 season.

Fulton took his Number 12 jersey and snatched the starting quarterback position away from the Swamp Rat. "It was competition," Warren would later say. "I just had to be ready if my opportunity came."

It wouldn't come before the Alabama game. Fulton was performing adequately for an eighteen-year-old sophomore. Tennessee rolled over Army in the first game of the season 21 to 0 at Knoxville. Auburn came to town the following week. They weren't so kind. "The next thing you know I was throwing two interceptions to a tackle," Fulton laughed about it years later. "He just stuck his hand up and plucked one right out of the air. He tipped another and it fell back down in his arms. That basically contributed to the tie at 13."

Fulton and the Volunteers bounced back two weeks later against South Carolina. It was the third home game for the youthful quarterback as he led his team to a 24 to 3 victory.

The next Saturday would be the third one in October. Tennessee would play the defending National Champions on their home away from home in Birmingham. Fulton would get to see on the other sideline one of the coaches he had turned down in order to come to Tennessee. The Swamp Rat was on the travel squad and was next in line to be quarterback. He would get a peek at the Bear who had turned him down. They both would get to see a sophomore by the name of Stabler and a senior from Cleveland, Tennessee, in the person of Steve Sloan at quarterback for Alabama.

Alabama week was developing into a great celebration of anticipation for Volunteer fans. Their hopes were unusually high considering the factual situation. Alabama was coming off a championship season—the second since Bryant came to Alabama as coach in 1958. Tennessee had not beaten the Tide since 1960. Alabama did have a blemish on its 1965 record when it lost the opening game to Georgia by a point. Otherwise there was not much realistic room for optimism among Vol supporters. But when were fans ever expected to be realistic?

Contrary to what some Tennessee fans thought then and may think now, the world did not come to a stop during Alabama week with its entire attention directed to the clash between the Orange and the Crimson.

During Alabama week of 1965, Lyndon Johnson was in the hospital recovering from gall bladder surgery. He would later show the scars to anyone who asked, or did not ask, to see them. It was at least a diversion for the President from the Vietnam War protests that were beginning in earnest.

For several years, Alabama week coincided with the World Series. On Thursday before the struggle of the football powers in Birmingham, the Los Angeles Dodgers won the Series in seven games with a 2-0 victory over the Minnesota Twins. Sandy Koufax pitched the three-hit shutout.

There was, in fact, the overlapping of three ball seasons as the basketball Vols opened practice on Friday of Alabama week in preparation for a December 1 tipoff. Coach Ray Mears was pictured in the Knoxville *News-Sentinel* standing on a chair in order to look eye to eye with Red Robbins and Tom Boerwinkle. Bobby Hogsett and Howard Bayne lent an imposing air to the photo.

On Clinton Highway in Knoxville, Clayton Motors was advertising a 1957 T-Bird, "a collector's item," black finish, convertible with floor shift for $2195. Or just down the street at Rebel Motors, a 1965 Mustang 2+2, automatic, 289 V-8, yellow with black interior, "a little jewel" could be purchased for only $2595.

The Tide was made a nine point favorite early in the week and then by week's end before the game a ten point pick. Both Knoxville newspapers featured stories on the Vols' defense and the emergence of a fine pair of linebackers in Frank Emanuel and Tom Fisher. Emanuel was the team leader and acting captain on the defensive side. Both were six feet three inches in height and weighed in at 215 pounds. Emanuel was described by the *News Sentinel*'s Tom Siler as a "dark-visaged dark-haired boy more likely to be scowling than smiling." Fisher was "blond, boyish, and quick with a quip."

Bear Bryant, never one to understate the meanness or fierceness of an upcoming opponent, described the pair as "the best linebackers in the conference."

Coach Dickey said, "Frank is playing football the way you like to see it played. It's hard to find a boy who has worked harder than Frank to be a better player."

On the offensive side, Ed Harris of the Knoxville *Journal* brought out the similarities between the 1965 squad and the 1928 team that had relied on the "Flaming Sophomores." The backfield of Tennessee had sophomores Fulton at quarterback and Walter Chadwick at tailback. Austin Denney was a sophomore end.

Senior Captain Hal Wantland was now described as U-T's "Mr. Block." His blocking in the game with South Carolina had allowed Fulton, Chadwick, and Ron Jarvis to eat up yardage running. Wantland had not carried the ball a single time in that game. He had started at quarterback in 1964 before moving to blocking back or fullback in Dickey's scheme of things.

Dickey had nothing but praise for his captain. In speaking of Wantland's unselfishness and desire at quarterback in the preceding season the coach said, "The single characteristic he exhibited that I'll never forget was that after throwing a pass, he ran downfield to throw a block to help spring a receiver. How many quarterbacks have you ever seen do that?"

An ad running on the sports pages in one of the Knoxville papers read: "Fix broken dentures at home in minutes. Amazing new Quik-Fix repairs broken plates, fills in cracks and replaces teeth like new. Fast! Easy to use! No special tools needed."

Perhaps Tennessee tackle Bill Cameron had not seen the ad, or perhaps he didn't need it. Possibly, some of the Alabama players might need the help of QUIK-FIX after the game if they played across from Cameron.

Anyway, after several hundred students gathered for an impromptu pep rally at the end of practice on Thursday, Senior Cameron was chosen by the team to speak to the rally crowd along with Gerald Woods. "I can't talk very plain. I don't have my teeth in. We'll do the best to make you proud," Cameron said.

And that was what the Tennessee coaches had prepared the players to do. Assistant George McKinney had given a lecture to the Vols. "Those Alabama guys believe they are going to win, not just this week but every week. You can see it in the way they walk. They think the fourth quarter belongs to them."

Despite the enthusiasm by fans and players, most newspaper writers picked Alabama to continue its dominance. Typical was Tom Anderson of the *Journal*: "Alabama over Tennessee—It's just impossible to believe that the Vols are so far ahead of schedule as to be able to humble the defending National Champions."

The travel squad consisted of fifty players. They left in time to have a light workout on Legion Field on Friday. Tennessee would wear orange jerseys, Alabama red. It was the clash of autumn colors before the NCAA stepped in and said the visiting team had to wear white jerseys.

The coaching staff had to be concerned about Alabama's offense. Despite having lost Namath to the pros after the 1964 season, Alabama had a couple of dandies in Steve Sloan and Kenny Stabler. Sloan was a senior and Stabler a sophomore. Fulton and Stabler, both of the same class, would share the same jersey number—12.

Sloan, the recruit from Cleveland, Tennessee, had first played on defense and then moved over to offense when Namath was hurt. Bryant did the same thing with Stabler. Stabler was playing safety until the coach moved him over to back up Sloan.

"We're looking for a quarterback who can play the first three quarters. Sloan has done a tremendous job in the fourth quarter, but we want to move the ball and score some before the fourth period," Bryant said.

Looking back on his first game against Alabama from a perspective of about thirty years, Fulton said, "It was pretty scary going into Legion Field. It was a big crowd. A lot was riding on the game. I remember big games in high school, but nothing really compared to that one."

What about the coaching staff? Was Alabama just another game? Fulton smiled at the questions. "Well, I think they wanted to give us the impression they took it as one more game. I'm sure they tightened up a bit." He laughed. "It was a big game, especially when you go against Bear Bryant."

Defense, kicking, field position, fumbles, and the clock all played important roles in this titanic struggle. Scoring only occurred in the second quarter and after time had run out for the half. One drive by each team accounted for the scoring. There were missed opportunities on both sides.

It wasn't Fulton against Stabler or Fulton against Sloan. It was two good football teams against each other. The hitting was hard and clean—eight fumbles and only one penalty (five yards for Alabama being offside).

Neither team was able to get beyond the other's forty yard line in the first quarter.

Toward the end of the first quarter and going into the second, Alabama began to put together a serious drive with Stabler at the controls. He engineered a series of five first downs. "The nimble soph had runs of three, eight, five, three, four, six and six before Naumoff and Mack Gentry chilled him good on a rollout," according to Marvin West's account in the *News-Sentinel*.

Stabler and Sloan alternated at quarterback for Alabama. Stabler was mainly the running threat and Sloan the passer. Fulton did both for Tennessee.

Tennessee took over on its own thirty about midway through the second period when the drive of Alabama sputtered. Doug Archibald blocked an attempted field goal which Al Dorsey recovered.

Fulton and company then took over. The sophomore quarterback threw one to Wantland for twenty yards. Fulton then used his wild steer moves as he rolled left, turned back inside, got a block, and gained twenty more down to the Alabama 28.

He misfired on his next pass, ran for five on second down, and then found his summer buddy from the Tellico camp, Johnny Mills, for thirteen to the Tide 10. Stan Mitchell rumbled down to the one on a pitchout. He was given the ball again and muscled it in for Tennessee's only touchdown.

Alabama answered with a drive that covered the last 72 yards in less than a minute and a half. Stabler ran and Sloan passed. Dennis Homan caught. Alabama used two timeouts. They took the last one with just a tick left on the clock in the second quarter. Sloan sneaked in as time ran out. The half ended with the score knotted but with the Tennessee team shaking its collective head at how fast Alabama moved on them over the last two minutes. Momentum had shifted to the Crimson Tide. Stabler still hadn't thrown a single pass.

Coming out in the third quarter, Alabama seemed to take charge. But each time they threatened, Tennessee was able to turn them away. A sixty-six yard drive got them to the one-yard-line. Again, Stabler and Sloan shared the quarterbacking on this drive. Sloan was the one who fumbled on the one-yard line with Frank Emanuel recovering.

Fulton led his team out of the shadows of its goal post with

42

a fifteen yard run. Mitchell about matched that with thirteen of his own. Fulton fumbled, and Alabama recovered to thwart the drive.

Opening the fourth quarter, Tennessee's Jackie Cotton, who had an excellent day punting, put one out on Alabama's one-yard line. This gave Tennessee its best chance to score again when Alabama was unable to move deep in its territory and punted.

From the 42, Fulton ran eight, then three, before Chadwick lost the handle on a pitchout for a loss. Another loss of three on a sack set up a screen pass to Austin Denney for a gain of eleven. David Leake's field goal try of thirty-four yards was short.

Alabama started another drive that to Tennessee faithful looked as though it was inevitably pointed toward six points. Sloan threw to Ray Perkins for twelve. Sloan to another receiver for four as Tom Fisher made a great stop.

Sloan to Dennis Homan netted fourteen. A sack didn't stop the passing barrage of Sloan. The senior quarterback had passed his team all the way to Tennessee's four-yard line. A dive off right tackle took the ball to the two. Sloan bobbled the next center snap, and it was recovered by Naumoff at the seven.

Sloan had not participated in the thousands of snaps at Tellico with Johnson and Fulton. Stabler, the sophomore, had yet to throw a pass.

Tennessee was unable to move, but Cotton boomed a punt from his foot like a howitzer for fifty-eight yards.

Alabama had sixty-five yards to go and three minutes, twenty seconds left in the game. Considering what they had done at the end of the first half, Tennessee fans knew there was too much time remaining.

Sloan started at it again, forgetting the two fumbles that had kept them out of Tennessee's end zone. He tossed fifteen yards to Tommy Tolleson. After Doug Archibald pinned him for a one yard loss, Sloan hit Wayne Cook on third down for eleven. It was a first down at the Tennessee forty.

Derrick Weatherford made a big stop. But with a minute and a few ticks left, Sloan found Tolleson on a sideline slant to the middle for twenty-eight yards to the ten. A dive took the ball to the eight. Then a pitchout went wild and the Tide lost ten to the eighteen.

On third down Stabler and kicker David Ray reported with just thirty-four seconds left. Tennessee had the receivers covered, and Stabler ran for fourteen yards to the four. Tennessee cornerback Jerry Smith tackled him just before he could get out of bounds to stop the clock.

What happened next was one of the weirdest plays in the Tennessee-Alabama series.

Did Stabler think he had picked up a first down with his fourteen-yard run? He came in on third down with the ball on the eighteen. But it had been first and goal from just inside the ten.

Fulton later said, "I was surprised at what they were doing on offense. There was a question of strategy right there at the end."

Stabler was determined to have his first and only pass of the game. He quickly called a pass play in the huddle, took the snap, opened to his left, and threw the ball out of bounds.

Fulton saw it from the sideline. "He opened to the left and threw it out there. He was left handed. He just opened up and let it wing. Holy Moley! I knew it was our ball then."

He killed the clock with six seconds left, but unlike the first half, Alabama didn't have another play left. It had been fourth down.

The Swamp Rat was watching from the sidelines also. "I couldn't figure out what he was doing. Bear Bryant couldn't either. They could've kicked a field goal and beat us ten to seven."

To Stabler's credit, he didn't let the error affect his future performance. He was later voted co-quarterback of the century for Alabama with Joe Namath. His pro career speaks for itself of a highly skilled competitor.

However, when Al Browning wrote *The Third Saturday in October* a few years ago, he was in error when he said: "After taking possession at its 25-yard line, the Crimson Tide, behind the brilliant passing of quarterback Ken Stabler, moved it to a first down inside the Tennessee 10-yard line."

There was nothing "brilliant"about Stabler's passing on that third Saturday of October. He only had one attempt the whole day, and it was incomplete. It handed Tennessee the tie.

Two Tennessee boys passed that day. Charlie Fulton completed five of seven for 74 yards. Steve Sloan, from Tennessee playing for Alabama, threw for 205 yards on 13 completions out of 18 attempts. Stabler was the leading rusher for Alabama with 82 yards. Fulton led Tennessee with 66 yards.

Fulton didn't get to meet Stabler, Sloan, or Bryant after the game. In perhaps the understatement of his career, Fulton explained, "I think they were probably a little upset with the whole situation. It was a moral win for us."

Of the 70,000 or so fans at Legion Field, ten thousand were celebrating and the remainder were wondering what had happened.

To Doug Dickey, it said that the Volunteers "were back in the hunt."

Alabama had an enormous yardage advantage over Tennessee but could not put it into the end zone when there were opportunities.

Bryant said the disorganization was all his fault. "Tennessee is improving. They've got a fine team. They're going to be tough."

Sloan spoke about his fumbles, but there were no quotes from Stabler. There was little for him to say.

The Knoxville *News-Sentinel's* Tom Siler wrote that "Tennessee turned the football corner on this 7-7 tie."

Tennessee took over the ball and took the tie to the dressing room as a win.

Marvin West of the *News-Sentinel* wrote that, "Tennessee sophomore Charlie Fulton did everything you can expect of a young man facing Alabama for the first time."

Indeed, the whole Tennessee team had taken the talk of George McKinney to heart. They were learning what it was to be winners. Even in this tie, they knew they were the winners.

Excitement and euphoria reigned the remainder of Saturday night and all day Sunday.

Tragically, the team and all Volunteer fans were brought back to the real world, to life and death, early the following Monday morning. The car in which three assistant Volunteer coaches were riding was struck by a train in west Knoxville. The Volkswagen was mangled and pushed a hundred feet down the track.

Had the young coaches been recounting the Alabama game? Planning on how to build on their team's performance? No one would ever know.

Bob Jones and Bill Majors were killed instantly. The driver, Charlie Rash, clung to life for a couple of days before succumbing. Jones was the oldest at thirty but the one who had just four months before joined Dickey's staff. Majors had played ball for U-T in 1958-60. His brother, Johnny, had played before him, and his brother, Bobby, would follow.

Fulton still feels the emotion when he talks about it. "You go from a pretty big high to a serious low. I was in the dorm when I heard about it. They were all real young."

Dickey was just leaving home for the office when he got word of the horrible accident. He organized people to go to each home of the young coaches to take the news to the wives. He went himself to Bob Jones' house. "Bob was new here. He hadn't met many people. It was a very tough time for a lot of people. There were three young widows and seven children involved."

The football team and staff were a family of about a hundred members. "It's a traumatic event to any organization of a hundred people or so," Dickey explained.

With the team, Dickey had to attend to their feelings and yet prepare for another game on Saturday. "I told them that it was a tragic accident but that life was going to go on for the rest of us."

The team, staff, and community pulled together to comfort the families and yet "go on with life," such as it was, under the circumstances.

Houston came to town the next Saturday amid the drapings of sadness and mourning.

Fulton continued to quarterback the team during 1965 until he injured his ankle in the Mississippi game. He would only start one game as quarterback after that.

Those who knew Fulton during his quarterbacking days always describe him as a gifted athlete. According to Dewey Warren, Fulton, "was a great scrambler. He was probably a better runner than passer."

"Charlie was a great athlete, a great leader. He had good speed, quickness, and toughness. He darted and dodged and was hard to tackle," was the way Bill Battle would later describe him.

"His biggest asset was his ability to scramble, to maintain balance, and to run," Bubba Wyche observed.

But Charlie Fulton was unselfish, too. He would return in coming seasons as the tailback doing what he did best. In short, Fulton developed his abilities and gifts as far as he could and contributed to a fine start to the modern tradition of the THIRD SATURDAY IN OCTOBER.

1965

LINEUPS

	TENNESSEE	ALABAMA
LE	Denney	Perkins
LT	Bird	Duncan
LG	Woods	Calvert
C	Jellicorse	Crane
RG	Gratz	Fuller
RT	Lowe	Dowdy
RE	Mills	Cook
QB	Fulton	Sloan
HB	Chadwick	Thompson
HB	Wantland	Tolleson
FB	Mitchell	Bowman

SEASON RECORDS

TENNESSEE

21 ARMY	0
13 Auburn	13
24 S Carolina	3
7 Alabama	7
17 Houston	8
21 GA Tech	7
13 Mississippi	14
19 Kentucky	3
21 Vanderbilt	3
37 UCLA	34
BLUEBONNET BOWL	
27 Tulsa	6

ALABAMA

17 Georgia	18
27 Tulane	0
17 Mississippi	16
22 Vanderbilt	7
7 Tennessee	7
21 Florida St	0
10 Miss. St	7
31 LSU	7
35 S Carolina	14
30 Auburn	3
ORANGE BOWL	
39 Nebraska	28

GAME STATS	Tennessee	Alabama
First downs rushing	6	11
First downs passing	4	11
Total first downs	10	22
Attempts rushing	35	61
Yards gained rushing	135	193
Yards lost rushing	14	37
Net yards rushing	121	156
Passes attempted	7	19
passes completed	5	13
Passes intercepted	0	0
Net yards passing	74	205
Total yards gained	195	361

Quarterback stats	Fulton	Sloan	Stabler
Passes attempted	7	18	1
Passes completed	5	13	9
Passes intercepted	0	0	0
Net yards passing	74	205	0
Rushing attempts	15	--	19
Net yards rushing	66	--	82
Total yards	140	205	82

Clock Giveth, Taketh Away as Vols Withstand Tide

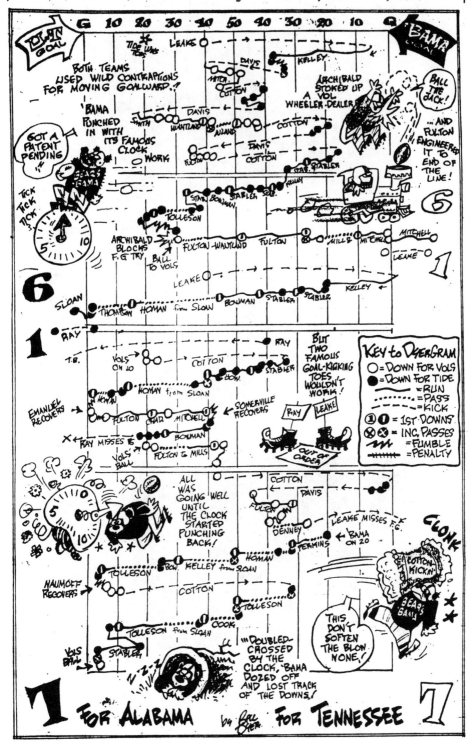

FOR ALABAMA by Bill Neal FOR TENNESSEE

LEGACY OF THE SWAMP RAT

At Tennessee

Charlie Fulton

Assistant Coach at Florida
(Courtesy University of Florida News & Public Affairs)

His address and passing statistics for the Alabama game are the same.

Chris Cawood

Why Football?

In one of the first battles of the Civil War, the ladies came out in all their finery and the congressmen in their top hats and suits to watch the Union Army knock back the Southern rag-tag band of rebels.

The Northern name for the battle was First Bull Run. The South knew it by First Battle of Manassas.

With picnic baskets sitting on red and white cloths, their bonnets adjusted properly, and their beaus on their arms, the ladies sat in the new grass beneath spreading limbs of old oak trees to watch the show below in the vale.

The Southern boys, however, would not cooperate. They insisted on fighting like a bunch of rascals who intended to win and ruin the picnic atmosphere for the society folk of Washington. The Union Army, along with the social elite, had to retire to the city post haste in order to avoid a total rout.

That was before football.

This American game is closer in analogy or metaphor to war than any other sport played.

In the other two great American ball games—baseball and basketball—all the players on a team do essentially the same things although there is a bit of specialization. Baseball players all throw, catch, and bat (except the pitcher in the American League). Basketball players pass, dribble, and shoot.

Football is more specialized. Offensive linemen are the

51

equivalent of tanks. Wide receivers are the air force to which the quarterback delivers "bombs." All linemen are "down in the trenches" for "hand to hand combat." Quarterbacks are the on-field captains, leaders, or generals for the offense. Usually a middle linebacker assumes that role on defense. Head coaches are the Five-star Generals of the sidelines.

Football is the only one of the three team sports that actually encourages and expects physical contact of a more or less violent nature. In baseball and basketball contact between bodies is only supposed to be "incidental" and not intentional.

Territory is important. The field is divided into "our" and "their" sides of the 50-yard line. Goal-line stands in essence protect the "home land" from invasion.

If one state's best team beats another state's best team, the victory can instill a sense of pride, happiness, and well being into the citizenry of the entire state of the winner and can make the losers feel like prisoners of war.

Remember when Goliath and David were sent out onto a battlefield to decide the battle for their respective armies? Perhaps that is one of the reasons for the great interest in football today. The players are representatives of the people. Fans get more worked up about Alabama week sometimes than the players.

Football has consistently had a higher attendance per game than the other two sports. "Sure," someone might say, "that's because they build bigger stadiums for football." Of course, the answer is that they build bigger seating capacities because there is a greater demand.

The ladies with the finery (much of it in Tennessee Orange) and the gents with the suits still come out to watch the combat. Now it is limited to the field that is delineated every five yards with a white stripe. The uniforms are brightly colored, the drum and bugle corps play "Rocky Top," and the players all wear combat helmets for the THIRD SATURDAY IN OCTOBER.

1966-The Swamp Rat

After the Bear had visited Savannah in 1962, Dewey Warren, the Swamp Rat, finished out his senior season at Jenkins High waiting for an opportunity to go to a big college. His team just missed the state championship playoffs by one game.

Dewey wanted to go to Georgia. "All my friends left to go to Georgia, but they didn't recruit me. Wally Butts was the coach. I think he had made the statement that I couldn't play college ball."

The Bear looked that afternoon in 1962, but he didn't go after the tough kid who could play linebacker or quarterback. Dewey still respected him. "Bear Bryant came over and watched us practice all day. He recruited in Alabama and not much out of state. A great guy."

He could have stayed on the south side of Savannah where he grew up. He had spent many a day along the creeks, rivers, and marshland near the ocean. "If I wasn't playing ball, I was crabbing or doing something on the water."

Another gifted athlete, he played ball in all seasons. And when he wasn't playing, he would slip away to explore the dark waters and deep, lush growth that was populated with not only fish, but the animals of the night that made spooky noises to boys in their early teens. A flat boat with a couple of lanterns and two or three adventurous boys aboard provided hours of escape from everyday life.

Dewey's family lived in a nice area of south Savannah. His

father was a sales representative for Gulf Oil for forty years. His mother was busy with Dewey and his younger brother.

"We lived out south. Next to the water. It was kind of like a little island with the river nearly surrounding us. I was on the water a lot."

He was on the water so much that his high school coach accused him of being late for practice one day because of his being on the river.

"Where you been, Dewey? Out riding the swamp buggies? On a boat? You're just like an old swamp rat!"

Of course, the other boys heard it. It stuck. Dewey Warren became the Swamp Rat as a high school sophomore. He was later to wear the name with pride when he became Tennessee's first pure passing quarterback.

As coincidence would have it, the name was applied to him by a Tennessee graduate himself. Lamar Leachman played center for U-T during the 1952, 1953, and 1955 seasons. It was through coach Leachman that the Swamp Rat ended up at Tennessee.

Leachman, as a former Volunteer, would naturally have pointed any of his players with a desire to play for a good program toward Tennessee. Except in 1962 and 1963, Tennessee was still running from the single-wing formation, and Dewey was a quarterback.

When Bear and Butts didn't show an interest in Leachman's quarterback, the coach turned to an assistant coach at U-T who had relatives in Savannah. Bob Woodruff, who in 1963 would move up to acting athletic director before assuming the role permanently, saw possibilities in the hard-nosed quarterback who doubled as a linebacker.

The Swamp Rat made his visit to Knoxville and liked what he saw. He was ready to get away from the flatland and marsh for a while. "I liked the mountains and the area. I liked the people. And I figured one day, they might switch from the single-wing to the T formation which would have been to my advantage."

As a freshman in 1963, Dewey watched the varsity struggle

54

through a year that would end the head-coaching career of Jim McDonald.

The freshman season was a roller coaster ride. The freshmen won two and lost two. They lost 6-21 to Georgia Tech; won 47-0 over Virginia Tech; won 27-10 over Vanderbilt; but lost 0-70 to Kentucky. The last loss still stands as the worst defeat of any Tennessee freshman team in the history of U-T football.

The good news and the bad news came with the same announcement in December 1963. Tennessee would finally go to the T formation. They would not do it under Jim McDonald.

For any player, when there was a change of system and change of coach in the same stroke, there was uncertainty. Would the new coach look for a talented quarterback from the ones already on board? Or would he recruit the quarterback he wanted? And a third question had to hang not only on the tongue of the Swamp Rat but on that of every freshman player: How much talent was there on a freshman team that couldn't score a point against Kentucky and allowed 70?

The answers were quick in coming. Doug Dickey signed seven quarterback prospects in the signing period of early 1964. He was high on Charlie Fulton from Memphis. However, all these prospects would be freshmen and therefore ineligible for the 1964 varsity season. The Swamp Rat would still have his chance.

It wasn't to be though. Less than ten days into fall practice, Dewey Warren disappeared from the quarterback depth chart and was sent to the scout team as a redshirt. Dickey had decided to go in 1964 with one of four players who had varsity experience at some position although none of them had played quarterback in college.

George Cafego, who had played on the great Neyland teams of 1937, 1938, and 1939, was the coach for the redshirts that made up part of the scout team in 1964. The Swamp Rat remembers his advice. "If you ever get your chance, take advantage of it. Be ready to play when you're called on. Take advantage and do your best."

Dewey took the lesson to heart and worked on both sides of the ball on the scout squad. If he couldn't be a quarterback, maybe he could be a linebacker. It was fun to hit someone anyway.

His call never came in 1964. He watched Joe Namath on a bad leg riddle the Tennessee defense as Alabama rolled 19-8 on the third Saturday in October. He was determined to be ready in 1965.

Competition. That's the way Dewey Warren described the battle to be the quarterback in 1965. "Charlie Fulton was a great scrambler. He wasn't very big. He was a better runner than passer."

Was he discouraged that he wasn't the starting quarterback at the beginning of 1965? Discouraged, no. Determined, yes. "It's just like anything else. You compete. Only one quarterback can play at a time. Football is a team sport anyway."

He would later look back on it and compare it with the way things are today. "You've got to be able to take the ups and downs. If you have to sit on the bench, you've got to understand that and accept it. Work harder to play. A lot of kids leave college because they can't accept it. They've been the top dogs in high school and they don't understand this."

The Swamp Rat was into his third year at U-T and had not started a game. However, he had to take some satisfaction in the fact that he had moved from out of nowhere in 1964, to second—just behind Charlie Fulton—by the starting game of 1965. As a team player, he supported both those who were ahead of him and those behind. He could think of the shape that Bubba Wyche was in and be thankful. Bubba had undergone his second knee operation and would miss the whole season.

Dewey never had an injury to amount to anything up to this point. He didn't mind the contact but rather relished the idea of opposing linemen coming in and him brushing them off. He could

56

do it in practice. Someday he knew he would get his chance for real.

When Fulton opened with an impressive performance against Army and a passable grade against Auburn, Dewey realized that the sophomore from Memphis had established himself as the quarterback for that year. He watched and learned. At the Alabama game in Birmingham, he watched three great quarterbacks in Fulton, Sloan, and Stabler. He saw how a mistake could cost a game.

Despite the tragic wreck the following Monday morning, and perhaps because of rededication after it, the team moved on through the next two games with steady resolve. The young Vols rolled over Houston 17-8 and Georgia Tech 21-7.

The following week, playing Mississippi at Fulton's home town of Memphis, the young quarterback went down with an ankle injury. He would miss practically the remainder of the season except for the Bluebonnet Bowl game.

The Swamp Rat got his chance because of the injury and never again turned the job back over to anyone on a permanent basis. He followed precisely the advice of Coach Cafego: "If you ever get your chance, take advantage of it."

In the three previous years, Mississippi had beaten Tennessee by a combined score of 69-6. In 1965, Fulton, Warren, and crew made it close—but still a loss—at 13-14.

Dewey settled into the quarterback role over the next two games as Tennessee steamrolled Kentucky 19-3, and Vanderbilt 21-3.

Then came the game for which the Swamp Rat will long be remembered. Tennessee had never played UCLA before 1965. They were not in the conference, being a west coast team. But by the time of the game, Tennessee had been selected to play in the Bluebonnet Bowl, and UCLA was going to the most prestigious bowl of all—the Rose.

The game was dubbed the "Rosebonnet" and has to rank among the ten most exciting games of all time for Tennessee fans. UCLA had Gary Beban, who would later win the Heisman trophy, at quarterback. Tennessee had the Swamp Rat who had been ignored by Bear Bryant and even his in-state school of Georgia. Except for an injury to Fulton, Dewey would have been watching the game from the bench.

Fulton traveled with the team to Memphis for the game even though he couldn't play. It was his hometown, and it was the last game of the season except for the bowl game. He enjoyed it. "It was a barnburner. Back and forth."

Dewey "always wanted to outdo the other quarterback." It was so much back and forth that it was evident the last one to score would be the winner. Touchdown met touchdown. Pass dueled with pass. Elbows were introduced to chins. Beale Street's rocking was nothing compared to the emotions within the stadium and of those listening to the radio account of the ebb and flow of the game.

Tennessee finally prevailed 37-34, and UCLA's coach, Tommy Prothro, never got over it. It was the first of a sporadic series that continues even to today. The winner of the UCLA-Tennessee game usually receives much media attention. This game in 1965 reestablished Tennessee as a national contender and put the "Big" into "Orange Country."

"Big Orange" was not regularly applied to the football team until 1966. Having originated with Ray Mears and the basketball Vols, the terms were still giving sportswriters trouble knowing when or when not to use "the" with "Big Orange" or "Big Orange Country."

Writing about a Tennessee football loss in early 1966, Ed Harris, Knoxville *Journal* sports editor, wrote: "There is no defeatist gloom in the Big Orange Country." Later, it became generally acceptable to use "the" with "Big Orange" but not with

"Big Orange Country." So much for the niceties of language.

Tennessee players were no longer just Orangemen or Volunteers. They would henceforth be the Big Orange and the surrounding environs would be Big Orange Country.

The Swamp Rat threw for three touchdowns in 1965 and ran for four, and he would come into the 1966 season as the starting quarterback even though Fulton had recovered from his ankle injury and Bubba Wyche had successfully rehabilitated his knee.

Tragedy struck the football team again at the end of spring break in 1966. Tom Fisher, who had played so well at linebacker along side Paul Naumoff in 1965, was killed in a car crash on the way back to school from Florida. The wreck, south of Knoxville on Highway 411, also took the life of another promising prospect in John Crumbacher. Gerald Woods, who had finished his eligibility, was injured.

The Swamp Rat and Tennessee started just where they had left off the previous year.

They beat Auburn in a shutout 28-0 for their first victory over the other team from Alabama in six years. Rice went down like a side dish 23-3. Then the week before Alabama, Georgia Tech surprised the strong Volunteers 6-3. Was looking ahead to Alabama reason for that loss? No one would comment.

During Alabama week in Knoxville, "Doctor Zhivago" and "Goldfinger" were still playing at local theaters. The Orioles were sweeping the Dodgers in the World Series. The Dodgers put up thirty-three scoreless innings.

Seating capacity at Neyland Stadium had increased to 54,429 with the addition of north end zone bleachers. Tickets were six dollars each.

Alabama came into the game having won three straight and allowing only seven points to be scored against them. Tennessee had allowed nine in three games. Defense would decide the game, most everyone predicted.

Both teams had good quarterbacks—Kenny Stabler for Alabama and the Swamp Rat for Tennessee. Some were surprised to learn that Tennessee was actually throwing the ball more than Alabama. Stabler had completed 26 of 32 for four touchdowns. Warren had connected on 47 of 76 for five touchdowns.

Going into the Alabama game, Warren would only need five passing attempts to break the school record held by Hal Littleton with 81. Johnny Majors held the touchdown passing record for U-T at that time with eight for the season. Warren would break several records by the end of the season.

He had quality receivers. Among those in 1966 were Johnny Mills, Austin Denney, Richmond Flowers, and Walter Chadwick. "So, probably if I had to pick one or two guys that I would go to in a tough situation, it would be Mills and Denney. Austin was so big, and he could get up over the middle. I always knew where he was," he would say years later in thinking back on his receivers.

Bill Battle had just arrived in 1966 to coach the receivers. He liked Flowers speed. The world-class speedster drew double coverage more often than not and allowed Warren to go to other receivers who were more open.

On the other side, Alabama was just as threatening. Coach Doug Dickey said he doubted "there is a quicker quarterback in America for ten yards than Kenny Stabler. He has more tricks on the option play than a magician."

Stabler's targets when he threw were Ray Perkins and All-American Dennis Homan.

Stabler and Warren presented a contrast in styles. Stabler ran more and only passed when the run wasn't there. When the Swamp Rat ran it was more by way of necessity than planned excursion. He would rather sit in the pocket, brush aside rushing linemen, and throw darts downfield.

So, the stage was set. Orange, Sugar, and Gator Bowl

representatives would be present to appraise both teams. *Sports Illustrated* would cover the game. Students spent the night in sleeping bags outside the ticket office at Alumni Gym earlier in the week to be in line for tickets. The largest crowd ever assembled in Tennessee—over 56,300—would witness the game.

Dark and ominous clouds loomed over Shields-Watkins Field as fans filed in early to witness the last battle with Alabama on real grass in Neyland Stadium for twenty-eight years.

By game time, the clouds were no longer threatening but were pouring a steady rain. The coin toss could be decisive. Alabama won and took the south goal to defend. Tennessee elected to kick rather than receive. After six plays, Dickey's decision to kick placed him with the great thinkers like Socrates, or perhaps with the great gamblers, as Alabama fumbled and Derrick Weatherford recovered on the Bama 22-yard line.

Fulton, now at tailback, scampered to the nine-yard line. Flowers caught a Warren pass for two yards. Another running play gained one. Then the Swamp Rat found the receiver who he "always knew where he was." Big No. 84—Austin Denney—caught a short pass to the right side and ran it in for what would be Tennessee's lone touchdown of the day—and Warren's sixth of the year. Gary Wright converted the extra point and Tennessee led 7-0 with just a few minutes gone.

Alabama players began to look like mere mortals when they could not penetrate the Vols' side of the field on their next two possessions.

Fulton made another powerful run on the slippery field, leaving Crimson Tide players grasping at elusive shadows while they slid on their bellies in the muck. He put the ball on the Tide's 27-yard line. Three plays later, Wright kicked a 40-yard field goal to give Tennessee a 10-0 cushion.

During the next two quarters neither team scored although Alabama made it to the Tennessee seven-yard line before fumbling.

Ron Widby, the versatile three-sport All-American from Knox Fulton, kept the tide behind a seawall with his superb punting. He kicked for distance, for placement, and for hang time. One of the boomers sailed fifty-five yards.

While Alabama's offense wasn't being consistent in the first two-and-a-half quarters, the defense was trying to provide them opportunities. Finally, toward the end of the third, the Tide's defense recovered a Vol fumble that set Alabama up on the Tennessee 46-yard line. A holding call a play later gave the Tide the ball at the fifteen. Three plays later Stabler stepped in for the score.

Alabama went for the deuce and succeeded with a pass from Stabler to Wayne Cook as the final quarter got underway.

Tennessee couldn't move it in two possessions.

Alabama on their second try got a drive going. They rode the running of Les Kelley and the passing of Stabler to take the ball almost to the goal line before settling for a field goal that gave them an 11-10 lead.

With just three minutes and twenty-three seconds left, Dewey Warren and Company began their final drive of the day. Bill Baker made a sensational catch for twenty yards. On the next play, the Swamp Rat pitched out to Fulton who hadn't forgotten how to throw. He hit Denney with a pass over the Bama forty-yard line, and Denney lugged it on down to the 13.

Bob Mauriello carried down to the two for a first down. Neither the first down nor the second down plunge of Mauriello into the line gained anything. Mauriello hit the line, got stacked up, and bounced off to the right with the ball being placed on the right side hash mark.

Tennessee had another down left to get better field position, but someone or ones called timeout—U-T's last. Sixteen seconds were left. It wasn't enough to run another play and then get the kicker in. The Vols were forced to send Wright in on third down to try the kick from the bad angle.

The Swamp Rat was holding for Wright. The snap was good, Warren got the ball down and placed, Wright stepped into it. A hush enveloped the crowd of 56,300 as the ball took flight, turned end over end, and gained height, nearing the right stanchion of the goal post just twenty yards or so from where the Swamp Rat had placed it so carefully on the wet turf.

Somewhere on its flight to the left, the leather oval spheroid began to curl off to the right ever so slightly. In golf they call it a slice. It was air resistance, the rotation of the ball, the laces and seams, or something in the aerodynamics of objects moving against wind that then began to exaggerate the curl more and more.

Just as the ball passed that point on its zenith, and even with the right-side pole of the goal post in the south end zone, almost everyone looked for an answer to Referee Charles W. Bowen, who was paid to make such decisions.

Stationed directly behind the upright, Bowen gazed skyward as the rotating ball made a dark splotch similar to the outline of a raven against the gray sky. Bowen then flapped his arms down and in a crossing manner, bringing heartbreak to some 50,000 Vol fans in the stadium and countless others listening on the radio and joy to the Alabama fans in the northeast corner.

"Take the beak from out my heart, and take thy form from off my door!"

"Quoth the Raven, 'Nevermore'."

It was **NO GOOD, IT WAS NO GOOD!**

"I still say today that the kick was good," Dewey Warren said in April, 1994. "But, you know, once the official makes the call, that's it."

Gary Wright had put the Vols in position to win with an extra point and a hard 40-yard field goal earlier in the game. This time he missed, but he did not lose the game for Tennessee. They are team victories and team losses.

That was it for the Alabama game in 1966. Was it justice? Should Alabama have won the game in 1965 and Tennessee in

1966? Often the Tennessee-Alabama series does not turn out as players, fans, coaches, and sportswriters think it should.

The Swamp Rat and Tennessee went on to a successful rest of the season losing only one more time and gaining a trip to the Gator Bowl where they beat Syracuse.

Warren and Fulton did well in the Alabama game. Warren hit six of nine for 41 yards. Fulton was one for one for 38 yards. Fulton was the leading rusher for Tennessee with 51 yards, and Warren, who was faster and more elusive than he looked, had nineteen. Stabler was seven of fifteen for 72 yards.

In 1956, Johnny Majors set the single season record for touchdown passes with eight.

In 1966, the Swamp Rat totally erased that standard and set a new one of eighteen. That record would stand for twenty-seven years, until 1993. The young man who would break Warren's record in 1993 was Heath Shuler. Shuler was recruited by Johnny Majors.

Just what kind of quarterback was the Swamp Rat?

"Dewey was a hard-nosed player. A darn good passer. He made a lot happen with the passing game," according to Charlie Fulton.

Coach Dickey described the Swamp Rat this way: "He was a guy who was kind of a clumsy-looking sort of an athlete in some ways, but a guy who could throw the ball and get things done."

Bubba Wyche who would follow Warren observed him for several years. "His strength was that he had a great arm. He had leadership. Some might say 'cocky.' But it was a positive cockiness. He had a strong will which was a big asset for the team."

Dewey had this to say about how he saw himself: "You know, they'd talk about my speed, but it wasn't my job to run the ball. We had guys in the backfield to run the ball. Mine was to sit in the pocket and throw the ball. I could run when I had to run." However, in his career he had twelve touchdowns running the ball.

Asked about standing coolly in the pocket while linemen rushed toward and by him, Dewey said: "Once I got focused in, nothing bothered me. All I wanted to do was win. I didn't pay any attention to those guys coming at me. If I got hit, so be it. I didn't have rib pads, and half the time my chin strap wasn't buttoned. The helmet had just one bar."

Bill Battle sums up the Swamp Rat as well as anyone: "Dewey was a fun guy to coach. He was a great passer. Had superb confidence. He believed strongly in himself and everyone else. Dewey was a great leader. He was a great passer. He was a very average runner.

"But when he got in the huddle, everybody believed we were going to score. And, there wasn't any doubt we were going to win. Dewey exuded that kind of confidence. He would stand in the pocket and have somebody coming right in his face. He'd stand there and deliver the ball.

"Dewey was being interviewed after one game during the time when we could still wear the tear-away jerseys. Dewey always had seven or eight torn off him in a game. So, they were interviewing him after the game and he had stood in the pocket and taken a beating.

"They asked him about it, and he said, 'As long as I can stand on one leg and raise this arm, I'll stand in there and throw that ball.'"

That was the Swamp Rat.

Warren left the 1966 Alabama game believing he would have one more chance at Stabler and Alabama in 1967. It would then be time for settling up.

1966

	LINEUPS		SEASON RECORDS	

	TENNESSEE	ALABAMA	TENNESSEE	
LE	Denney	Cook	28 Auburn	0
LT	Boynton	Duncan	23 Rice	3
LG	Rosenfelder	Calvert	3 GA Tech	6
C	Johnson	Carrell	10 Alabama	11
RG	Gammage	Stephens	29 S Carolina	17
RT	Bird	Dowdy	38 ARMY	7
RE	Mills	Perkins	28 Chattanooga	10
QB	Warren	Stabler	7 Mississippi	14
HB	Fulton	Canterbury	28 Kentucky	19
HB	Flowers	Homan	28 Vanderbilt	0
FB	Mauriello	Raburq	GATOR BOWL	
			18 Syracuse	12

GAME STATS	Tennessee	Alabama	ALABAMA	
First downs rushing	8	9	34 LA Tech	0
First downs passing	2	5		
First downs by penalty	1	1	17 Mississippi	7
Total first downs	11	15	26 Clemson	0
Attempts rushing	37	57	11 Tennessee	10
Yards gained rushing	135	186	42 Vanderbilt	6
Yards lost rushing	9	14	27 Miss. St	14
Net yards rushing	126	172	21 LSU	0
Passes attempted	10	15	24 S Carolina	0
passes completed	7	7	34 S Miss.	0
Passes intercepted	0	0	34 Auburn	0
Net yards passing	79	72	SUGAR BOWL	
Total yards gained	205	244	34 Nebraska	7

Quarterback stats	Warren	Fulton	Stabler
Passes attempted	9	1	15
Passes completed	6	1	7
Passes intercepted	0	0	0
Net yards passing	41	38	72
Rushing attempts	5	12	18
Net yards rushing	19	54	56
Total yards	57	92	128

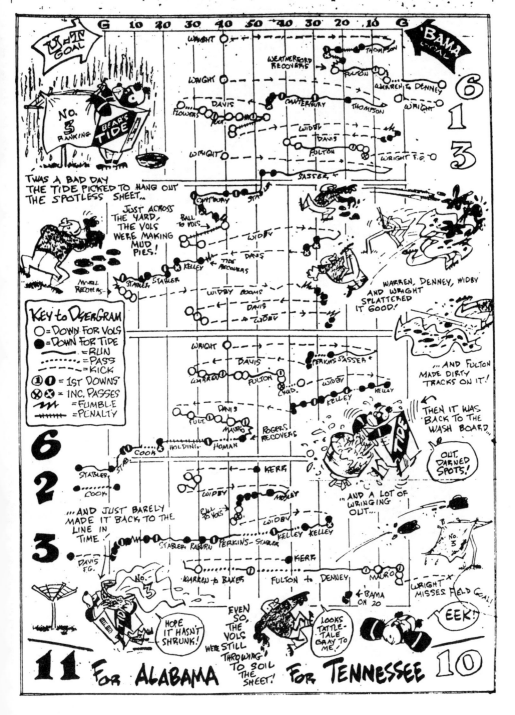

Dewey Warren meant business as quarterback for U-T
or now as a representative for Humbolt Express.

1967-Bubba Wyche

Sarah Wyche would stand and watch her younger son on the floor or in a chair before school. He would extend his left leg and stretch it. He would rub it, add a little weight, and continue the exercises the doctor had told him to do.

In January 1964, it was hard to look at his left knee, see the diagonal scar, and not cry. Physically, she knew he hurt, but emotionally she hurt just as much for a son to whom athletics meant so much. He would not play basketball or baseball his senior year of high school.

Ten plays in one football game had convinced the coach, Bubba Wyche, and his mother and father that surgery was necessary to repair the knee.

The injury had come on a freak play during pre-season practice in August. He was running an option play in scrimmage with his own players from his quarterback position. Going down the line, he was ready to pitch when he saw that his option man had run the wrong direction. There was nothing to do but to turn it upfield and gain as much as he could.

Although it was just practice, Joseph Murry Wyche Jr. intended to get what he could. The plant of the leg against the ground and subsequent hit did in the anterior cruciate ligament of his left knee. He tried to rehabilitate it short of surgery, but the knee kept on hyperextending.

The one game he tried it in had convinced him. Even though he completed seven of eight passes for three touchdowns in the ten plays, his season was over. Perhaps his career.

"Bubba," as his fifteen-month-older brother Sam called him, grew up in the Buckhead area of Atlanta and played all three seasons of ball from age seven on up. His father traveled for Dairy Queen to set up retail outlets. Sarah Wyche was a secretary at an interior design company and a full time mother.

It was a nice neighborhood but not affluent. The four lived in a two-bedroom house with one bath. The family was close-knit and so was the neighborhood.

"The one thing I can remember my entire life all the way back to the days I can't remember was being on the athletic field. Football, baseball, or basketball. Whatever was in season," Bubba would later recall.

His athletic talent blossomed in all three. His baseball team traveled regularly to Havana to play the best Cuban youth. Even as a twelve-year-old, he was already being noticed. Pitching for his little league team, he set a world's record by striking out all eighteen batters to face him in the six inning game.

Bubba wasn't big then—about five feet tall and a whopping eighty pounds. His little league football team won the state championship. Pretty heady achievements, considering they had to play the teams of Valdosta to win.

In high school, Bubba continued the three sports. By the time he was a sophomore at North Fulton High School, he was an accomplished quarterback. He beat out a senior—his brother Sam—for the starting job.

It was during that year that colleges began to write to him. They were interested in a strong-armed quarterback with touch. Southern California, UCLA, Texas, Alabama, Georgia, South Carolina, Georgia Tech, and Tennessee were among the forty colleges nation-wide that showed an interest. The Chicago Cubs looked at him for a pitcher.

When he finished his junior year, he was named All-State

70

in football, basketball, and baseball.

Then came August and the knee injury. October brought the surgeon's knife and a cast to wear for three months. January arrived miserably with a shriveled leg and a bright red scar along the inside of the knee.

Not many teams or coaches were still interested in pursuing a high school senior whose main knee ligament had been severed and had to be reconstructed. The Chicago Cubs were gone. The letters from colleges with football programs stopped coming. Some wrote a "sorry to hear about that" note.

Sure, he had an excellent junior year. But how much could you count on a young man who didn't get to show his stuff as a senior and who would be months in rehabilitation? It was too risky for many. Alabama was among those that completely backed off after the injury.

Dreams for a young boy had been so easily made. They were pursued with vigor, determination, and will power. Then just as he was beginning to realize them, they were snatched from his grasp and disappeared faster than the burst of colors from fireworks on the Fourth of July.

It was enough to make a person cry, give up, or find excuses for quitting. But if Bubba Wyche did any of the three, nobody knows about it. Instead, he worked out three times a day with the exercises the doctor prescribed and more. If there was one college that would take a chance on him, he would be ready.

There was one. Tennessee and coach Vince Gibson were still interested. Gibson came in with Dickey and kept the contact alive with Bubba that had been started under Jim McDonald and others.

Florida State, South Carolina, and Georgia were others who would take a chance with the talented quarterback. Bubba eliminated Georgia from contention as he had always been a Georgia Tech fan.

Tennessee and Knoxville were just right. They were out of state but close enough that his mother and father could watch him if he got to play.

Walter Chadwick from nearby Decatur visited Tennessee at the same time, and they both signed. Chadwick was a tailback. Bubba was one of seven quarterbacks signed by the new regime. They told him it would only be a one-year deal to see if his knee could withstand college athletics. He took it. He would make his dreams come true despite the knee injury.

In 1964, Bubba took his turns alternating at quarterback with Charlie Fulton and Albert Dorsey on the freshman team.

His knee continued to strengthen with his exercise program. During the organized winter workouts, the coaches noticed Bubba's athletic ability and decided to move him to the defensive backfield where he had played some in high school.

Just as he thought he had put his knee injury behind him, it buckled on him again two weeks into spring practice of 1965. He missed the remainder of spring practice hoping the knee would heal without further surgery.

When two-a-days started in August, the knee just could not take the pounding. While Fulton was running the team at quarterback, Bubba was resting, waiting to make a decision on surgery. In October he had the second surgery on his left knee. Tennessee and Alabama tied 7-7 in Birmingham with Bubba Wyche back in Knoxville. He was redshirted for the season.

His aspirations to be Tennessee's quarterback looked to be lost dreams. In the spring of 1966, Bubba was back in the defensive backfield. The Swamp Rat had wrested the starting quarterback position to himself when Fulton had gone down with his ankle injury.

Bubba wasn't even on the same side of the practice field now. "As I stood there on the defensive field, I caught myself so often putting myself on the offensive field. I wasn't a hundred per cent involved mentally in the defensive activities."

Apparently, somewhere along the way, the coaches noticed the same thing. It was not a time that a player could be so forward as to suggest that he would rather play offense than defense. But

72

when pre-season practice began in August, Bubba found himself back on offense.

However, he was nowhere near pushing Warren out of the quarterback slot. "At that time, I was on the outside looking in. We had an awful lot of good athletes at the University of Tennessee. Unless you got the right break, you might be a good athlete and not ever see game time."

He quarterbacked the scout team to help the varsity prepare for opponents.

His varsity playing time in 1966 didn't require much ink to summarize. He carried the ball three times for a net loss of eight yards. He passed six times with two completions for a net gain of eighteen yards.

Despite the paucity of statistics that could be favorably viewed, Bubba entered the 1967 campaign with a shot at being the backup to Warren. In fact, he moved to that position in pre-season awaiting the opening game with UCLA.

This time it was not his left knee that put him in the hospital but his right side. He had an appendectomy after an attack. Rehabilitation didn't take as long as with his knee surgeries, but still he had lost his place at the feeding trough.

Tennessee lost its first game to UCLA in Los Angeles by a 16-20 score. There were two weeks to prepare for Auburn.

Shug Jordan brought an Auburn team to Knoxville that he felt could beat Tennessee. However, the Swamp Rat drove Tennessee down the field with four passes plus a 20-yard run by Walter Chadwick in the opening drive and the Vols were back aiming for victory.

Then in the third quarter, Warren was helped from the field after a knee injury. Charlie Fulton came on in relief and performed as he had in 1965 before the ankle injury. Tennessee won 27-13 with Warren completing eight of twelve and Fulton five of ten. Fulton rushed for 103 yards while Warren had twenty-seven.

Georgia Tech was just two weeks off. The Vols had another week off to prepare for a game without the Swamp

73

Rat—the first in nearly two years. Fulton was able and ready. He played more at quarterback in the Auburn game than he had played all of 1966. Bubba moved back up to second.

With two weeks preparation under their belt, the Vols and Coach Dickey felt confidence return, Fulton at the throttle. The senior quarterback would get his first start of the season at quarterback.

In the first quarter, Fulton completed three of four passes and rushed for twenty-nine yards before a shoulder and helmet to his rib cage sent him to the sidelines and then to the hospital.

Bubba Wyche, the kid from Atlanta who lived near the Georgia Tech campus, would get his first real varsity action against his hometown school. Ironically, the same things that had kept him back in the competition—a knee and a pain in the side—led him to be the quarterback when Warren went down with a knee injury and Fulton with a broken rib.

While Fulton was being helped off the field, an unusual thing took place. Bubba had never taken any snaps from the starting center and All-American Bob Johnson. So, Dickey persuaded the referee to allow Wyche to take a couple of practice snaps from Johnson during the injury break-in-action.

After a fairly shaky start, Bubba threw two touchdown passes to Richmond Flowers, and the Vols went on to a convincing 24-13 win. Fulton was out indefinitely. Warren would not be ready for Alabama the next week. Bubba Wyche was named Southeastern Back of the Week for his efforts.

However, Alabama lay ahead down the road in Birmingham. How would the junior quarterback react to getting the first start of his career against nationally ranked Alabama, senior Kenny Stabler, and Coach Bear Bryant?

Dewey Warren, the old Swamp Rat, so much wanted one more shot at Alabama that he pushed his recovery and started working out with the second offensive unit. He told anyone who would listen that he would be ready.

Folk singer Joan Baez was jailed in Oakland, California, after a war protest during Alabama week in 1967. Sidney Poitier and Rod Steiger were the lead actors in the movie "In the Heat of the Night" that was playing at the Riviera in downtown Knoxville. Elizabeth Taylor and Richard Burton starred in "The Taming of the Shrew" at the Capri two miles from U-T's campus.

Bob Gibson was named most valuable player in the World Series as the Cardinals beat the Red Sox in seven games.

Ray Mears and Stu Aberdeen opened Vol basketball practice with a sixteen-man varsity squad that included, among others, Bill Justice and Billy Hann.

Alabama was ranked sixth and Tennessee seventh going into the week. The Tide was picked by six and a half points to win.

Although it was accepted that Tennessee had improved and become a well-rounded team under Coach Dickey, there were questions as to how far the coach could dip into his quarterback ranks and be successful.

Ben Byrd of the Knoxville *Journal* wrote on Monday of Alabama week: "Like everyone else, I am left wondering what effect the possible loss of both Warren and Fulton would have on the Tennessee-Alabama game, if it comes to that. It is a rare thing, indeed, for a team to reach down to a third QB and continue to function at its normal pace, and yet off his performance against Tech you would have to say that Bubba Wyche can do the job."

Tennessee's balance included the running of Richard Pickens at fullback and Walter Chadwick at tailback. With a new quarterback at the helm, their load would be even heavier. Receivers like Richmond Flowers, Kenny DeLong, and Gary Kreis could help a good quarterback look spectacular.

The runners had help from an offensive line that included Bob Johnson, Charlie Rosenfelder, John Boynton, and Joe Graham.

On the defensive side, Tennessee had a pair of sophomore linebackers who had been showing great promise. Steve Kiner and

Jack Reynolds could plug holes and squash runners almost before they had gotten the handoff.

The defensive backs who would take on Alabama's tandem of Kenny Stabler and Dennis Homan included Albert Dorsey, Mike Jones, and Jimmy Weatherford.

Alabama led the series 23 to 19 as the Vols left for Birmingham and the fiftieth meeting between the two teams.

Bubba Wyche was somewhat overwhelmed by the attention he had received since the Georgia Tech game and the importance of the upcoming clash with Alabama.

"The newspaper reporters and ones for *Sports Illustrated* were knocking on the door and ringing the phone. Then, when we went down the following week to Birmingham, we walked onto Legion Field, and I looked across at this bigger than life living legend. I get chill bumps even saying it today. There he stood—Paul 'Bear' Bryant. I was absolutely devastated."

He looked into the stands and wished his parents could have been there. Of course, just a few weeks before, he was a third-string quarterback with no hope of even playing in the Alabama game, let alone starting. His parents had told him to sell his tickets to have a little extra spending money. The two tickets he was given and the four others he could purchase went a long way in helping to supplement a college junior's needs.

Now, this would be a sellout with over 72,000 present and no room for his mother who had suffered with him long hours through his knee rehabilitation.

His attention was drawn back to the field and across the way where Kenny Stabler was warming up with tosses to Dennis Homan.

"I watched them warm up. I started feeding off of that. The more I participated in the pre-game activities, the more energy I felt. My desire and confidence increased just as though they were feeding off the aura of Legion Field and the day."

Was he ready to start the first game of his career? He thought so.

A little earlier Jimmy Dunn, the offensive coordinator, had tried to lighten the atmosphere for his quarterback: "Bubba, you know, last week you were able to win Southeastern Back of the Week. All you've got to do this week is go down there and beat Alabama, and Stabler, and Bear Bryant."

"He was trying to be funny, but it wasn't working that way," Bubba said later.

Saturday, October 21, 1967, dawned as a beautiful day. The sky brightened to a bright blue with the sun making it warm to the fans and players. Orange jerseys were ready to meet red. Helmet straps were buttoned and jock straps checked. Alabama wanted to avenge the 7-7 tie that occurred on the field two years before, and Tennessee knew they should have won the last time out when the field goal was missed. The Swamp Rat was suited up on Tennessee's sideline.

Tennessee took the opening kickoff and immediately tested the Alabama defense. It was a next to perfect drive. Pickens, the Knoxville Young High School product, carried twice for near ten yards each time. Bubba passed to Flowers and then to Chadwick for sizeable gains. From the one-yard line, Chadwick punched it across. Karl Kremser kicked the extra point.

Alabama was unable to get more than one first down on its opening drive. They punted.

Tennessee stalled and punted.

Alabama was then able to muster a 51-yard drive for the tying score.

Neither team was able to score the remainder of the first quarter or the entire second quarter, although Jimmy Weatherford disquieted the Tide with an interception of a Stabler pass. They went to the dressing rooms at halftime knotted at 7-7 just the way the game had ended two years before.

After an exchange of possessions at the opening of the third quarter, Tennessee got a break when a poor Alabama punt followed the Tide's second possession.

From the Alabama 40-yard line, Tennessee began its next drive. The Vols could smell elephant blood waiting at the goal line. Bubba found his touchdown friend of the week before—Richmond Flowers—for a nine-yard gain. Pickens blasted for a first down at the 30.

Bubba, not one to desert a good thing, tossed to Flowers again who took it to the eighteen. Bubba ran for two and Pickens for six.

Then from the ten, Bubba started left, pitched back to Chadwick at tailback, and then delivered a block that took the linebacker out of contention to contain Chadwick. Kenny DeLong had sneaked unnoticed into the left side of the end zone. Chadwick threw a left-handed knuckleball into the cradling arms of DeLong for the touchdown. It was Chadwick's first pass of his career at Tennessee. The Swamp Rat held for Kremser's extra point and Tennessee was ahead 14-7.

Later in the third period, Mike Jones snatched another Stabler pass before the men in red could get their hands on it and ended up at the Vol 46-yard line.

Bubba showed that he could still run on a twice-repaired knee when he went up the middle after finding no one open on a passing call. His friend from Decatur, Chadwick, gained another twenty-two yards to the 24-yard line of the Tide. After a loss of six and two incompletions, Kremser came on to attempt a forty-seven yard field goal.

The Swamp Rat held, and it was good. Tennessee 17, Alabama 7.

Alabama had always laid claim to the fourth period. It was ready to begin. This time it would belong to a young man named Dorsey who turned twenty-two on the day of the game.

The fourth quarter opened as though the magic was still there for Bryant and the Tide just as it had been the year before when the unseen finger had nudged Gary Wright's field goal attempt off course.

Taking the ball on their own seven-yard line after a 60-yard punt by Alabama, the Vols lost a yard on first down when Bubba was sacked while looking for a receiver. On second down, disaster struck when Mike Dean, from Chadwick's hometown of Decatur, Georgia, intercepted Bubba's pass and returned it to the sixteen. Four plays later the Tide scored to close the gap to 17-13.

They went for two on the conversion, but young Jack Reynolds, with the help of Jimmy Weatherford, broke up Stabler's pass to Homan.

Tennessee could not move the ball after the kickoff and punted. Once again the Tennessee-Alabama series would come down to who had the best defense in the fourth quarter. On second down, Kiner blitzed and threw The Snake for an eleven-yard loss.

The next play was no better for Stabler. He passed, Mike Jones deflected, and Al Dorsey intercepted.

Tennessee ran three innocuous plays and punted. Herman "Thunder Foot" Weaver did better this time with the help of Richmond Flowers. The punt bounced near the goal line but was batted back toward the ten before entering the end zone. It saved Tennessee about ten yards. Rick Marino and Vic Dingus continued to pressure Stabler from their defensive line positions.

Stabler's passes began to grow eyes as he found receiver after receiver open in the Tennessee secondary. But he went to Albert Dorsey's side again when he shouldn't, and the birthday boy had his second interception of the fourth quarter.

Tennessee couldn't move and punted again.

Alabama took over 70 yards away from Tennessee's goal with two minutes left in the game. All Alabama needed was one touchdown. With Stabler's arm, they had time to do it.

Homan was briefly open at the Tennessee 20-yard line but just could not make the catch. Stabler went to Richard Brewer for twelve and a first down. Dingus got through and wrapped Stabler up for a twelve-yard loss on the next play.

Stabler couldn't resist going to Dorsey's side one more time. He should have. Dorsey cut in front of the intended receiver, took the ball, and raced into the end zone making it 23-13 and erasing the spectre of Alabama domination.

The Swamp Rat trotted onto the field to hold for the extra point. It was Tennesee's last offensive play. It was the last time that Dewey Warren would touch the ball against Alabama. The injured quarterback from Savannah had done his part—whatever it took—to say "No" to Alabama, Stabler, and Bear Bryant.

Coach Dickey was carried to the middle of the field to meet Coach Bryant. Among the Tennessee players shaking hands with the "living legend" was Bubba Wyche.

When Sarah Wyche, Bubba's mother, started to think about missing the game, she had decided to go and take her chances with getting a ticket. A mother had to do what a mother had to do. Bubba's father couldn't go, so his mother rode to Birmingham with some friends.

There she went from gate to gate trying to find a ticket or a way in. The gatekeepers had heard all kinds of stories over the years from people trying to get into Legion Field when it was sold out. Her requests were met with polite cynicism. "No Ma'am, we don't have any tickets. You can't go in without a ticket."

The lady in the red dress started early in her pursuit of entry and never gave up. Finally, taking her wallet out, she showed a gatekeeper her driver's license. "See, my boy is starting at quarterback for Tennessee. I've got to get in!"

The gatekeeper looked, took pity, and waved her in. "You'll have to stand if you can't find a seat. We're all sold out." It didn't matter. She was in. She got to see her boy complete eight of fourteen passes and rush for twelve yards. He had helped Tennessee win in his first start.

When the game was over, Mrs. Wyche found Mike Jones who helped her to find Bubba. It was one sweet embrace.

Tennessee had intercepted Stabler five times. Dorsey had three of his own. He made Southeastern Back of the Week and, later in the year, All-America based partly on his performance against Alabama. Jimmy Weatherford had an interception as did Mike Jones. Jones made the cover of *Sports Illustrated* with him hitting Dennis Homan.

It was Alabama's first loss in twenty-six straight starts. Tennessee was going up the ladder of football supremacy in the South while Alabama was taking a brief respite.

Bubba Wyche got the victory he wanted but the following week returned to back-up quarterback behind the Swamp Rat where he remained the rest of the season.

The Vols went on to win all of their remaining regular season games and ended up rated second behind USC and O.J. Simpson in both the AP and UPI polls which were taken before the bowl game with Oklahoma.

The third-ranked Sooners won the battle in the Orange Bowl by a score of 26-24 in a game where it was all Oklahoma in the first half and all Tennessee in the second.

For Charlie Fulton and the Swamp Rat, it was the end of their careers at Tennessee. Neither one had ever made an All-America list or All-SEC as a player. They just hung in and did whatever it took to make their teams into winners.

When Fulton was in the hospital after suffering the broken rib in the Georgia Tech game, Ben Byrd wrote these words about him in the Knoxville *Journal*: "Charlie Fulton should not be allowed to lie out there in that hospital without being told what a remarkable football player he is. . . .

"The thing he does best, it seems to me, is to get away from that defensive pressure quickly. . . .

"Because of this latest injury, one of the Vols' alltime greats will probably wind up without his name embellishing the All-SEC lists."

Fulton was, and is, more than a football player though. His academics landed him on the Academic All-SEC in 1965 and 1967. He also maintained his well-rounded personality by singing with the U-T Singers. He played baseball his senior year.

Charlie Fulton went straight through his eligibility without a redshirt year. He graduated on time with his class in Business Administration.

He was drafted by Boston in the sixteenth round but decided to sign with Edmonton of the Canadian Football League instead. He started at quarterback and was named Rookie of the Year. He stayed two years before coming back to U-T to Law School.

However, in 1970 when Doug Dickey took Florida's head coaching job, he called on Fulton for help. He went first as a graduate assistant and stayed for nine years. He coached the freshmen, was head recruiter, and finished as academic advisor during his years with the Gators.

Fulton decided against going with any other football program after Dickey left Florida. He had been with Dickey for four years in college and nine as an assistant which was a big chunk of his life.

However, his loyalty and industriousness still show. He has been with ZEP Manufacturing for the past fifteen years as a sales representative. He makes his home in Gainesville just a mile or so from the Florida campus. He still sings for the local choral group in Gainesville. His son, Chad Fulton, will be a junior at U-T in the fall of 1994.

Fulton usually sees the Tennessee-Florida game in person. He won't disclose who he'll be pulling for except to say he favors orange.

Asked to sum up the Tennessee-Alabama rivalry, Fulton had this to say: "I think it was a game that people looked at as not only a very pivotal game of the season, but a very heated rivalry. It was a game that the players keyed toward winning, maybe even more so than any team we played. And the fact that Bear Bryant was there made it as though you were not only playing the Alabama team, but you were playing Bear Bryant too."

Dewey Warren finished out the 1967 season at quarterback. He led Tennessee to the highest regular season finish it has attained since the Vols went from the single-wing to the T. The Big Orange finished No. 2 in both the AP and UPI polls.

The Swamp Rat went to the Cincinnati Bengals in 1968 and started fourteen games but was cut the next season when a couple of other quarterbacks came in. One of them was Sam Wyche, Bubba's brother, who hadn't done too well in high school competing against his sibling but went on to a pro career.

Not deterred, he went to the Las Vegas Cowboys of the new Continental Football League. He was described in a news story as an "exciting and scrambling type of ballplayer that ignites the Cowboys every time he steps onto the field. He is quickly becoming a favorite in Southern Nevada as fans flock to the hometown games to watch his gambling type of play."

He forsook professional football after a couple of concussions and other pesky injuries and returned to U-T to help with the freshman team when Bill Battle became coach.

In 1972, he went to Brigham Young and helped install a passing offense. From there, he went for a short stay at Kansas State.

He couldn't stay away from Tennessee. He came back to coach the Copper Basin High School team and then to Sewanee to be offensive coach. He stayed there for seven years, helping with the football team and coaching the baseball team.

Now, he's back to his adopted home of Knoxville where he has been a sales representative for Humbolt Express for six years.

The Swamp Rat has two daughters. Angela lives in Orlando and Monica is a sophomore at U-T.

He was surprised in 1994 that his record of eighteen touchdown passes in a season had stood for twenty-seven years. "We didn't throw the ball that much. We had a great running attack and a good defense. With all the great quarterbacks that have come through here, and as much as they've thrown the ball, I'm amazed the record lasted as long as it did."

The Swamp Rat's coaching philosophy was the same as his playing: "I always said competition makes you better. Only eleven can play at a time. You always had to be ready. If something happened to the first teamer, the guy coming in had to be ready to play."

That's what stands out about Dewey Warren. He came to Tennessee when it was still a single-wing institution. Amid a change in coaches, he kept his head and his dedication. He was prepared to step in when he got his chance.

When he was injured in 1967 and couldn't personally lead the Vols into Birmingham, he supported the one who could and did what he could. That amounted to holding for Karl Kremser's extra points and field goal.

But he did his part. And when he saw that final extra point sailing through the uprights to make the score 24-13, there was no one happier than the Swamp Rat or prouder of a team that had come so far during his years as a Volunteer.

On a cool October afternoon in 1967, a tourist strolling by Room 388 of the Gatlinburg Inn in the Tennessee mountain town heard the strumming of a guitar coming from the room. He stopped and listened for a moment.

"OK, how's this? 'Rocky Top, you'll always be home sweet home to me. Good Ol' Rocky Top, Rocky Top, Tennessee.'"

Career Statistics

CHARLIE FULTON

	RUSHING		PASSING		
	CARRIES	YARDS	ATTEMPTS	COMPLETIONS	TD'S
1965	118	298	59	29	4
1966	109	463	6	2	0
1967	69	328	19	12	0
TOTAL	296	1089	84	43	4

DEWEY WARREN

	RUSHING		PASSING		
	CARRIES	YARDS	ATTEMPTS	COMPLETIONS	TD'S
1965	47	121	79	44	3
1966	70	41	229	136	18
1967	45	0	132	78	6
TOTAL	162	162	440	258	27

Vols Give Tide the Snake-Rattle-Roll Treatment

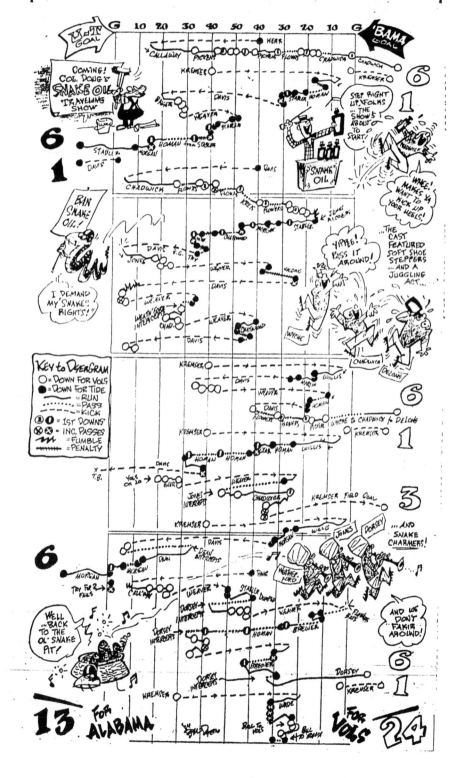

Chris Cawood

1967

LINEUPS			SEASON RECORDS

	TENNESSEE	ALABAMA	TENNESSEE	
LE	DeLong	Homan	16 UCLA	20
LT	Gammage	Reitz	27 Auburn	13
LG	Graham	Summerville	24 GA Tech	13
C	Johnson	Johnson	24 Alabama	13
RG	Rosenfelder	Stephens	17 LA State	14
RT	Boynton	Rustin	38 Tampa	0
RE	Dalton	Dixon	35 Tulane	14
QB	Wyche	Stabler	20 Mississippi	7
TB	Chadwick	Morgan	17 Kentucky	7
WB	Flowers	Willis	41 Vanderbilt	14
FB	Pickens	Chitwood	ORANGE BOWL	
			24 Oklahoma	26

GAME STATS	Tennessee	Alabama	ALABAMA	
First downs rushing	9	8	37 Florida St	37
First downs passing	4	8	25 S Miss.	3
First downs by penalty	0	1	21 Mississippi	7
Total first downs	13	17	35 Vanderbilt	21
Attempts rushing	55	46	13 Tennessee	24
Yards gained rushing	165	137	13 Clemson	10
Yards lost rushing	23	49	13 Miss. St	0
Net yards rushing	142	88	7 LSU	6
Passes attempted	15	32	17 S Carolina	0
Passes completed	8	15	7 Auburn	3
Passes intercepted	1	5	COTTON BOWL	
Net yards passing	92	154	16 Texas A&M	20
Total yards gained	234	242		

Quarterback stats	Wyche	Stabler
Passes attempted	14	32
Passes completed	8	15
Passes intercepted	1	5
Net yards passing	81	154
Rushing attempts	21	18
Net yards rushing	12	25
Total yards	93	179

Bubba Wyche was a youth baseball star who competed with brother Sam before becoming U-T's quarterback.

1968-Going For Two In A Row

Times, they were a changin'.

Up until the 24-13 victory over Alabama in 1967, Tennessee fans had been reasonably content with being "competitive." With the win, all that changed. Now conquest was expected. Fans were singing the praises of the still young Doug Dickey, and in their minds, putting Bear Bryant out to pasture.

It was contagious. Sportswriters became afflicted with penning about Bryant's near demise. Even before the 1967 game with Alabama, Ed Harris, the Knoxville *Journal* sports editor, wrote that "Bryant (was) in the twilight of a championship coaching career at Alabama."

Tom Siler, sports editor of the competing Knoxville *News-Sentinel*, wrote after the game: "Now, Bryant faces the sunset of a great and brilliant career in the field of coaching, having won championships at Kentucky, Texas Aggies, and Alabama. And he isn't likely to get another streak going, not at his age."

However, Tom Anderson of the Knoxville *Journal* didn't let one loss distort his view: "So Alabama dropped its first decision in 26 starts and already some are hurrying to bury Bear. . . 'The dynasty is dead. No more stomping around on water. A new era is born.' . . . I'd be a little slow about consigning the Great Rehabilitator to the skull orchard. . . He may now need water wings or skis for transportation in his old age, but to try to embalm him while he's still breathing could lead to embarrassment."

Future years would ultimately prove the wisdom of not pronouncing Coach Bryant done as a molder of championship football players and teams. It would be fifteen years before he would step aside as a legendary coach. He enjoyed the longest "twilight" and "sunset" ever known. His sunset and twilight stretched out farther than most coaches' careers.

With the entrance of 1968, Tennessee fans' appetites and expectations were high, whetted by the exploits of the Swamp Rat and Company in 1967. As the year progressed, football, as a diversion from the real world, became more precious.

The year was different—a watershed. It rushed in with the Tet Offensive by the North Vietnamese. Saigon was under siege.

It would be a Presidential election year. War protests beset Lyndon Johnson wherever he went. On the night of March 31, LBJ, in a nationally televised broadcast, withdrew from the race. Some thought it was a day-early April Fool's joke. It wasn't.

April brought the assassination of Martin Luther King, Jr. in Memphis. June bore the same news of Bobby Kennedy in Los Angeles.

August thrust into the homes of Americans by way of television the Democratic National Convention in Chicago where the police and protestors clashed. The police used truncheons and dogs against the heads and buttocks of those in their way.

After the convention, the voters were given the choice among the triumvirate of Hubert Humphrey, Richard Nixon, and George Wallace.

The populace cried out for relief, "When will football season begin?"

Even at Shields-Watkins field and within the football program, there were changes underway that would forever alter the appearance of football in Big Orange Country. One difference would be superficial, but the other would be deep and permanent.

Tennessee football would be first in two categories. No longer would the players cavort on real grass. Tartan Turf, an artificial grass, was put down on the field over the summer and would be ready for the opening game on September 14 with Georgia. It was hailed as the wave of the future. No fertilizer, no mowers, no mud, and low maintenance. The immediate cost would be offset in short order by the savings on upkeep.

Irvan B. Williamson, Wisconsin's athletic director and chairman of the football rules committee, predicted that within a few years "every football field in the nation will be covered with synthetic grass." His school also had just purchased a Tartan Turf field.

His prophecy was, perhaps, put in perspective when he also added: "There is a strong movement among coaches on the rules committee to restrict the free substitution rule. Some feel good football players should play on both offense and defense."

The other change in 1968 would be of much more significance.

Lester McClain was the first black player to suit up for a varsity football game in the Southeastern Conference. Tennessee was leading the way in race relations in athletics, and it would forever change the game. The exclusion of blacks from athletic competition with whites in the South had gone hand in hand with other types of segregation and had persisted longer.

Phil Fulmer graduated from Franklin County High School in 1968 and came straight to U-T. Lester McClain was a year ahead of him. Was race an issue at Tennessee? "No. I don't think that was an issue with anybody. It was more an issue with the press than anything. It was certainly a great compliment to Lester as to what he was able to do and how quickly he adjusted."

Were football players isolated or insulated from what was going on in the world? "No. I think everybody did a nice job of putting the priorities in order. Academics and football were very important, but we were also aware of the issues," Fulmer remembered in 1994.

McClain, a product of Nashville Antioch High School, came in as a freshman in 1967. Another great black athlete, Albert Davis, of Alcoa High School near Knoxville, was recruited but did not enroll. So McClain was left as the first and only black player in the 1967 class.

Bubba Wyche remembers it wasn't too easy for McClain. "With him being the first black player in the Southeastern Conference, he was subject to a lot of adversity with the racial slurs and the things that came along with those 1960's problems. We were very close friends."

Wyche, looking back on it, is somewhat thankful for his second knee injury that knocked him out of the 1965 season. Where would he have been if his knee had not been injured that year? "I would have been a defensive back in 1965 and probably for the rest of my career. I wouldn't have been there in 1968."

Instead, after showing what he could do in the 1967 Alabama game, Wyche became the starting quarterback in 1968. He is the only quarterback in Tennessee history to have played significantly on both natural and artificial grass.

What did he think about the change to Tartan Turf in 1968? "I was very excited because it was a field that was advertised as being perfect all of the time. It was to be perfectly flat, well drained, no divots or spike marks, and no bad places on the field.

"But, in practice, the carpet was so thick that it was easy to stub your toe and trip. It would make you look bad. We only had a couple or three hours practice on it before the first game. We didn't have a big advantage over Georgia.

"After I got used to the Tartan Turf, I liked it. I felt quicker and as though I had good stability on it."

Everybody didn't like it. Opposing coaches in general, and Georgia's Vince Dooley in particular, thought Tennessee had the advantage with the new field.

If it made the quarterback quicker, the new surface was a

boon to the receivers. Coach Dickey's recruiters had early on began to wed speed and brawn. Players with world class track speed were brought in with the assurance that they could play football and run track.

One of the first of these speedsters was Richmond Flowers who was plucked from the back stoop of Bear Bryant in Alabama. Flowers was a high hurdler who had hopes of making the 1968 Olympic team until he suffered a bad pull in a hamstring.

Even the kicker, Karl Kremser, joined the Vols because he wanted to high jump for the track and field team.

Wyche remembers Flowers as "one of the fastest people in the world at that time. He had incredible speed."

Bill Battle was the coach of the receivers in 1968, and he thought he had lost Flowers to the Olympics and the injury. Flowers thought he would redshirt in 1968. He had to recruit him again.

"Look, man, you can't redshirt. We'll put you at tailback," Battle remembers pleading to Flowers. "That kind of excited him about playing tailback. So he came back out. He didn't know how to play tailback, but he could run faster than anyone on the option. Bubba knew how to run the play. I bet if we hadn't gotten Flowers back in 1968 we wouldn't have won six games."

The quarterback also had Ken DeLong, Gary Kreis, Bill Baker, Richard Pickens, and McClain that he could go to.

Two teams on the schedule in 1968 had players Bubba Wyche had faced in high school and was familiar with. Several young men from the Atlanta area now started for Georgia and Georgia Tech.

The Vols opener with Georgia was also the debut for the Tartan Turf. Neither team had an advantage. It ended 17-17 after last second heroics by Wyche and his receivers. It was 17-9 in Georgia's favor with just a second to go.

"I knew if I could look off Georgia's great safety, Jake Scott, I had a chance to hit Kreis on a down and end. It worked just like it was drawn up. We scored after the gun had gone off.

Then the try for two was with zero on the clock. Kenny DeLong came underneath after a two-count delay and bingo, a two-point conversion."

Coach Battle remembers the last-second touchdown play against Georgia was one that was drawn up on the sideline by Dickey and had never been used before by Tennessee.

Tennessee had two weeks before they played Memphis State in Knoxville. The Vols settled down and disposed of the pesky Tigers 24-17.

A trip to Houston allowed a little respite as the Vols downed Rice 52-0. A sophomore quarterback by the name of Bobby Scott made an auspicious appearance, throwing for two touchdowns and running for another after Wyche had retired to the sideline.

Wyche was hospitalized again early the following week. This time it was for cellulitis of the left forearm and abrasions of the left knee and elbow. This was his third time in the hospital since coming to Tennessee. He was getting to know the nurses on a first name basis. In a day he was out. Nothing would keep him from playing the next two games.

Georgia Tech preceded Alabama week as it had for the two previous years. Bubba Wyche would be going home to Atlanta to start against his hometown school.

On October 12, 1968, the quarterback, who would not have been at Tennessee that year except for a knee injury, and the first black player to wear the Tennessee Orange teamed up for a first that can never be taken from them. Bubba Wyche threw the first touchdown pass to a black receiver in the history of the Southeastern Conference. Tennessee won 24-7.

Alabama week began in earnest.

Richard Nixon, just three weeks from the November election that would send him to the White House, stopped in Knoxville on Tuesday of Alabama week to campaign. He was depending on a heavy Republican vote in East Tennessee to carry the state. He wouldn't pick a favorite in the Alabama-Tennessee duel. Hubert Humphrey had been at U-T earlier in the month.

Interest in Tennessee football had grown to a stage that there was talk about installing lighting for night games at Neyland Stadium. Tickets were up to $6.50 each. John Ward was in his first year of football broadcasts on the Vol Radio Network.

Denny McClain of Detroit and Bob Gibson of St. Louis went head to head in a pitching matchup in the World Series. The Tigers won the Series.

Apollo Seven was on its mission. The Dow Jones thirty industrials reached the 948.6 mark. Jackie Kennedy flew off to marry Aristotle Onassis.

The Olympics were underway in Mexico City. Ralph Boston won the bronze in the long jump after having won two golds in 1960 and 1964.

Tommie Smith and John Carlos gave their clenched-fist gesture at the award ceremonies of the Olympics after winning and coming in third, respectively, in the 200 meter race.

The east upper deck of Neyland Stadium had been completed, bringing capacity to over 64,000. Near that many showed up early on the third Saturday in October of 1968 to see if Tennessee could do something that no other team had done to Bryant's Crimson Tide—win two in a row.

The lineups for the game display how the game has changed over the past quarter century. The largest offensive lineman for Tennessee was Chip Kell at 228 pounds. For Alabama, the weight chart showed Paul Boschung, at 221 pounds, to be the largest on offense. Mike Hall, a 227 pound linebacker, was the Tide's heaviest defensive player. Frank Yanossy played right tackle for Tennessee and weighed in at 232.

Tennessee came in with a three-win, one-tie record compared to Alabama's three wins and a loss. The Tartan Turf was covered on Friday as a downpour soaked the area. Neither team worked out.

The sky was still threatening at time for the coin toss. Alabama won and tried to take the benefit of the wind, but the player pointed in the wrong direction.

The Vols scored their only touchdown of the day on the opening drive. Wyche ran on first down for eleven yards. Flowers went wide on the option at tailback for seven.

When the Tide stuffed the runs up the middle, Wyche tossed a short screen to Richard Pickens who rambled thirty-two yards from his fullback position, all the way to Alabama's six-yard line.

Now it was time for Flowers with first and goal. He ran wide for just a yard. Wyche called his number again, and Flowers got a tough three up the middle. It was a safe handoff. Why not try it again? They did. Flowers got to the one.

It was fourth down and the Big Orange was just a yard away. There was no deception. Flowers got it for the fourth consecutive time and slammed into the line and then into the end zone for the touchdown. The speedster from Alabama scored on a power play up the middle. He had just gone the toughest six yards in football. At 178 pounds, he got the ground with heart more than brawn.

Karl Kremser got the extra point out of Wyche's hold.

Alabama opened at their 22-yard line with two fullback thrusts into the middle. Then a Scott Hunter pass to Donnie Sutton gave them a first down.

Sophomore defensive back Tim Priest made a tackle on the next third-down pass by Hunter for minus yardage, and the Tide had to punt.

Tennessee's next series went nowhere, thanks to a jolting tackle by Sam Gellerstedt on Pickens.

A penalty on a punt and fumble that would have given Tennessee the ball deep in Alabama territory instead put the Tide on the Vol 41-yard line.

Hunter kept on throwing. He hit George Ranager for a first down, and the referee blew the whistle, nullifying a fumble recovery by the Vols after Steve Kiner had separated the split end from the football. Hunter kept and ran from the twenty-five to the seventeen-yard line. Tailback Pete Moore got a first-down at the fifteen.

Jimmy Weatherford, Bill Young, Neal McMeans, and Jack Reynolds plugged up inside and outside to where Alabama was stifled. Mike Dean kicked a 28-yard field goal. Tennessee 7, Alabama 3.

There was no more scoring by either team the remainder of the first quarter, or the second, or the third. As had often happened in the past, the October battle settled down to a defensive struggle. Who would get a break, a fumble, or an interception?

Hunter fumbled but recovered it. Bill Young intercepted a Hunter pass, but the Vols were unable to take advantage of it. Each team would have a successful offensive play or two until an error, usually forced by the strong defense, thwarted the drives.

When the fourth quarter opened and the teams changed ends of the field, the Alabama players held up hands with four fingers showing. They believed they owned the last quarter. Tennessee's players looked and responded with a strong drive.

Wyche started by running for eight. Pickens then got the first down. Bubba threw a pass in the flat to Flowers right in front of the Alabama bench. The speedy tailback ran within spitting distance of Coach Bryant as he made fourteen yards on the play.

Next, Wyche found the big, steady hands of Kenny DeLong for ten. A penalty set the Vols back. Bubba then saw McClain alone long enough to make a reception and get fourteen yards—a yard short of the first down.

The ball was on the 37-yard line of Alabama with almost ten minutes left in the game. Dickey decided to try a field goal with Kremser. With a seven-yard placement from center, the ball would be kicked from the forty-four. Ten more yards to the goal posts from the front of the end zone meant the attempt would be fifty-four yards. No one had ever kicked that far in the history of the Southeastern Conference.

Wyche was the holder. The snap was good. Bubba caught it and placed the ball with laces forward. The thump of instep against leather sounded good. He looked up and watched the ball arch through the uprights with room to spare. There on the forty-five-yard line, Wyche and Kremser did a dance of celebration for a record-setting kick that put the Vols up 10-3.

Alabama was also saving their best for last. They weren't able to move on their next series, but they weren't through. Tennessee drove to the thirty-eight. Dickey sent Kremser back in. If he could hit from fifty-four, why not fifty-five? Karl wasn't ready to break his own record, and the attempt came up short.

Alabama wasted another possession as though they had all day to catch up. Tennessee also failed to take advantage of a short punt by Alabama. The Vols drove to Alabama's thirty-six-yard line this time and sent Kremser back in for another go at it from fifty-three yards. For the third time within five minutes of the fourth quarter, the soccer-style kicker tried another field goal from over fifty yards. It also was no good.

With four minutes left, Alabama decided it was time to make the game interesting. From their twenty, the Tide rallied behind Hunter. He passed on consecutive downs to Donnie Sutton for thirteen and fourteen yards. He found Danny Ford for seventeen more that took the ball to Tennessee's thirty-six-yard line.

The sophomore quarterback then missed three passes to receivers who were covered closely by Weatherford and the other Vol defensive backs. He then found Swafford, his split-end, at the seven for a first down.

Alabama tried to punch it in on two running plays. They got to the four. Linebacker Steve Kiner hit Hunter and made his third-down pass go awry. On fourth down, Sutton made a great catch for the Alabama touchdown with a little over a minute left. It was Tennessee 10, Alabama 9.

Bryant sent in another quarterback, Joe Kelley, with a two-point roll-out pass play. Kelley was looking for Sutton again but there were to be no heroics on this play. The pass failed.

98

The Tide was forced to try an onsides kick which they successfully executed to the dismay of Big Orange fans. Alabama recovered at the Tennessee 47-yard line, and Hunter quickly threw to Ford for seventeen yards. In four plays, Bear's boys drove it to the 19-yard line and positioned the ball for a 36-yard field goal attempt by Mike Dean. Five seconds remained.

Senior defensive back Jimmy Weatherford did not want to see the Tide win on a last-second field goal in his last game against Alabama. He eased up from his cornerback position and switched places with Nick Showalter. He aligned himself where he could make a run and dive to where the ball would leave the ground at the point of the kick.

He was just far enough outside the end that he wouldn't be touched. He looked down the line at the ball, and with the snap, took off. In the second and a half or two seconds, he ran, extended his body, crossed his hands, and felt the thump of the ball as it went on its flight toward the goal.

Was it enough? Or had he just brushed it on its way to victory for Alabama? He lay on the ground for a second until he got the answer in the shouts of his teammates and sixty thousand Big Orange fans.

This time Alabama's last-second try was **NO GOOD**. Two years before, it had been Tennessee's field goal try that had just barely missed. Things were evening up.

Doug Dickey now stood even, toe to toe with Bear Bryant. After five years of competition, each had won two, lost two, and tied one.

Bubba Wyche had done nothing spectacular in the 1968 game. Just as in the 1967 one in Birmingham, he had made a run here, a pass there, a block for someone else, and held the ball for extra points or for Kremser's record-setting field goal. As a leader, he did what was necessary to win. He threw for a hundred yards, connecting on 13 of 22, and ran for a net of 13.

On the other side, Scott Hunter had thrown a school-record 45 times for 187 yards, all to no avail.

The Alabama game usually boiled down to basic football—tackling, blocking, and kicking—not theatrics or heroics by either quarterback. Lester McClain recalled one of those blocks. "I remember Ken DeLong coming back and catching Mike Ford from the blind side on a block. One of the best blocks I've ever seen in my life. I'm sure Mike remembers that well."

As for Bubba Wyche, McClain, now an insurance executive in Nashville, describes the Tennessee quarterback as being "full of confidence. He was probably the most confident guy that I ever played with. He just took total control of the ball club when he came in during the 1967 Georgia Tech game, and that continued through 1968."

Two weeks later, Bubba threw for 223 yards with 17 out of 24 completions against UCLA and a 42 to 18 win for the Vols.

Tennessee went on to an eight-win season and an invitation to the Cotton Bowl.

Bubba was not exactly rebellious, but it was his senior year, and he had a tendency to let his sideburns grow a little longer than Coach Dickey approved—almost to a sinful midway point of his ear. On Cotton Bowl picture day in Dallas, Coach Dickey looked over at his quarterback who had helped win two Alabama games and noticed the longer than preferred sideburns.

"Wyche, get your sideburns trimmed or get the next plane back to Knoxville."

Bubba smiles about it now. He got his hair trimmed. He wasn't going to miss the last game of the season after what he had been through.

In 1969, Bubba had to choose between trying the Atlanta Falcons who were bringing in six quarterbacks or going to Canada to play. He went to the Saskatchewan Roughriders. From there he went to Detroit and Chicago of the World Football League and stayed in football until 1975. Then, the league and his knees gave way at the same time. He had had three knee operations. He came home to Atlanta.

By May of 1994, Bubba Wyche's knees had been operated on nine times—seven on the left and two on the right. He underwent knee joint replacements in both knees in 1993. "I could actually do a complete knee bend for the first time since 1963."

However, the good fortune was not to continue. Five months after the operation, a dormant staph infection came alive in his left knee making it "swell to the size of a volleyball." The doctor checked it the next morning and had him on the operating table within hours. While he was under with an anesthetic, the decision was made to remove the knee joint and fuse the lower and upper leg together.

He woke up kneeless on the left side but thankful he had a leg and a life. He wears a built-up shoe on the left foot to help make up for the shorter leg. Bubba doesn't regret the fact that football brought him the knee problems. The relationships, memories, and good times that he had outweigh the physical problems he has suffered.

The Downtown Greenery is the business that he and a partner started in 1975 from the back of a pickup truck. They thought selling tropical, semi-tropical, and other plants would be "a good way to meet girls." They also could drive to the Florida Keys to buy the plants.

From a six-thousand dollar investment, Bubba has built the business to where it grossed over $1 million last year. He now is the sole owner. He has twenty-four employees and a fifteen thousand square foot greenhouse and warehouse facility on the northwest side of Atlanta.

Mainly doing interior plants for large buildings, he has among his clients the CNN complex and other large downtown buildings in Atlanta.

Bubba and his wife, Lindy, have two dogs and a cat.

Oh, by the way, Bubba's older brother, Sam, whom he beat out for the starting quarterback job at North Fulton High School, hasn't done too badly either. He walked on at Furman and became the quarterback, became an assistant coach at South Carolina, then a pro quarterback with Cincinnati, and later a pro coach, taking the Bengals to the Super Bowl. He is now the head coach of the Tampa Bay Buccaneers. His daughter, Kerry, is a junior at U-T.

The Wyche brothers only had to look to their mother for a prime example of true grit which she seems to have instilled in them. Sarah Wyche still lives in the Atlanta area where she can turn the pages of the scrapbooks and remember her sons' exploits. "Did you know that Bubba once pitched a perfect game? Yes, he struck out every batter who faced him," she told one sportswriter.

That third Saturday in October of 1967 will be one that will stay etched in her memory forever. Dressed in a red dress with a string of white pearls around her neck, she was the mother who tried desperately to get into Legion Field. Didn't they know her son was there and what he had been through? Then she got in and watched, filled with the pride that only a parent can contain, when her younger son took his turn as the quarterback for the Tennessee Volunteers.

She remembered all the days when Bubba lay on the living room floor, straining to lift the metal shoe until the veins stood out in his neck as though they would burst while he rehabilitated his knee. Now he stood dressed in orange and helped to put a dent in the armor of Alabama which, to that point, had been impenetrable.

Chris Cawood

1968

	TENNESSEE	ALABAMA
SE	McClain	Husband
LT	Stewart	Boschung
LG	Denbo	Ferguson
C	Kell	Grammer
RG	Rosenfelder	Samples
RT	Hollaway	Davis
TE	DeLong	Swafford
QB	Wyche	Hunter
TB	Flowers	Morgan
WB	Baker	Sutton
FB	Pickens	Jilleba

TENNESSEE

17 Georgia	17
24 Memphis St	17
52 Rice	0
24 GA Tech	7
10 Alabama	9
42 UCLA	18
14 Auburn	28
31 Mississippi	0
24 Kentucky	7
10 Vanderbilt	7
COTTON BOWL	
13 TEXAS	36

GAME STATS	Tennessee	Alabama
First downs rushing	9	5
First downs passing	3	13
Total first downs	13	18
Attempts rushing	46	39
Yards gained rushing	160	117
Yards lost rushing	27	20
Net yards rushing	133	97
Passes attempted	22	45
passes completed	13	19
Passes intercepted	0	1
Net yards passing	100	187
Total yards gained	233	284

ALABAMA

14 Virginia Tech	7
17 S Mississippi	14
8 Mississippi	10
31 Vanderbilt	7
9 Tennessee	10
21 Clemson	14
20 Miss. State	13
16 LSU	7
14 Miami	6
24 Auburn	16
GATOR BOWL	
10 Missouri	35

Quarterback stats	Wyche	Hunter
Passes attempted	22	45
Passes completed	13	19
Passes intercepted	0	1
Net yards passing	100	187
Rushing attempts	12	10
Net yards rushing	13	0
Total yards	113	187

103

Elephants' Hunter Bags 6-Pointer . . . but Not Vols

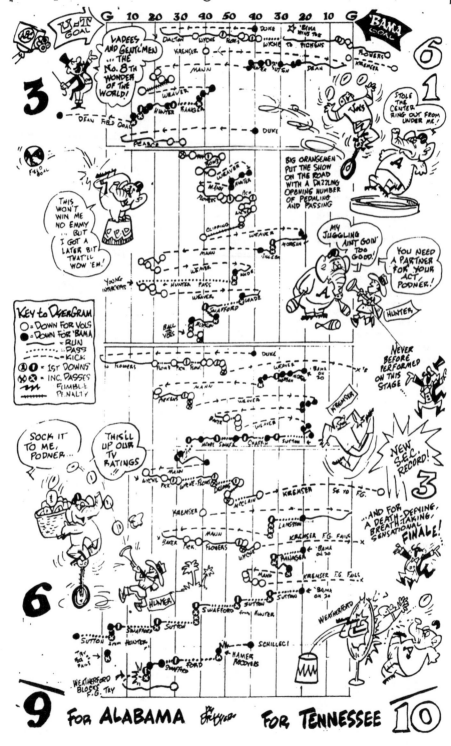

Career Statistics
BUBBA WYCHE

	RUSHING		PASSING		
	CARRIES	YARDS	ATTEMPTS	COMPLETIONS	TD'S
1966	3	-8	6	2	0
1967	62	141	69	37	4
1968	104	-37	237	134	14
TOTALS	169	96	312	173	18

Bubba let his hair grow in Canada.

Bubba Wyche passing the mantle to Bobby Scott (above) and with one of the plants he maintains in Atlanta from his Downtown Greenery (below).

Chris Cawood

Football Saturday

Ask football fans what they remember and like the most about the Alabama series (in addition to the football), and there might be a hundred different answers.

The pageantry, spectacle, color, sound, and aroma assault the senses from arrival near Neyland Stadium to departure after the game. It doesn't matter whether fans arrive by car, bus, airplane, or as one of the captains of the armada that makes up the Vol Navy. There's tradition etched into the pregame habits of fans who have been going to the games for ten, fifteen, twenty, or even fifty years.

The older ones might walk to the corner of Cumberland Avenue and Stadium Drive, look at the spot where Ellis and Ernest Drug Store stood, and reminisce about the hours spent there. A pregame meal in the student center, a walk on the hill to Ayres Hall, or waiting for the team to walk from their dormitory rooms to the stadium might be part of that tradition.

Boys selling newspapers with lineups on the front page, scalpers hawking tickets, souvenir stands, and the smell of hamburgers and hotdogs being cooked all fill the memories of anyone who has been among the ninety thousand or so on a Saturday afternoon near the stadium. Waiting while the band plays its way onto the field, pepping up the crowd along both sides of the street.

The Third Saturday in October is all the more special. The mountains are beginning to drape their trees with the colors of the participants—red and orange—in harmonious union, nature with man. There is a hint of fall in the air. The slant of the sun's rays is a bit different. A night or two has felt the cool air slide down from the mountains into the valleys along the river.

Inside the stadium in years past, there were the walking horses, the canon being fired from the northeast corner after Tennessee scores, the cheerleaders, and always the Pride of the Southland Band.

Dr. W. J. Julian, the band's director from 1961 to 1993 has seen it all. The band always traveled to Birmingham for the game with Alabama. Their fans were "very good."

"The Auburn fans were wonderful. I guess if you live in Auburn, you're glad to see anybody."

Dr. Julian "had a wonderful relationship with all the coaches." He saw them all from Bowden Wyatt through John Majors.

He began the famous "circle drill" in 1965 and has improved it since. The team running through the T formed by the band began in 1964, a collaboration between Coach Dickey and Dr. Julian.

The cheerleaders and Smoky are another part of the color. Mike Clift, now a successful lawyer in Cookeville, was captain of the cheerleading squad in 1968. Sarah Wyche was not the only one who had trouble getting a ticket to the Alabama game. Clift remembers arriving in Birmingham at Legion Field to find Tennessee "cheerleaders" already on the field in 1967.

"How many cheerleaders you folks have?" a gatekeeper asked as the squad passed through. Clift squinted into the sunlight and saw that the ones already there were not really cheerleaders at all but were fraternity brothers who had pilfered parts of uniforms from the closets of the real cheerleaders.

Anything to get entrance to the game that's played on the Third Saturday in October.

1969—Bobby Scott

"When I looked to one side of me and saw Jack Reynolds clenching his fists and gritting his teeth, and I looked on my other side and saw Steve Kiner with tears streaking down his cheeks, I knew that the Alabama game was something special."

What Bobby Scott was describing were not the effects of defeat or failure. He was picturing the scene as the Volunteers prepared to come out of the tunnel from the east side of Neyland Stadium onto Shields-Watkins field for the 1968 game with Alabama.

He knew the rivalry existed for several years prior to that 1968 game, but that was the first year that he was a varsity participant. It was the kind of intensity and fierceness in anticipation that each of the games with Alabama had spawned since 1965.

Growing up in Rossville, Georgia, just across the Tennessee line from Chattanooga, Scott was familiar with the series since the age that he could remember and had an interest in football. The Chattanooga newspapers' circulation included the Rossville area, and they carried the stories of the Vols' triumphs and defeats.

The next to youngest child among seven, Bobby was competitive from an early age. Ball—whether base, basket, or foot—was played with older brothers, the neighborhood kids, and schoolmates the year round. He became proficient in all. By high school, he had developed into a good catcher for the baseball team, a forward with shooting touch for the basketball team, and, by his sophomore year, the starting quarterback for the football team.

As a high school senior in 1966-67, Bobby was on a recruiting visit to U-T on the third Saturday in October of 1966.

"I had an old green poncho pulled around me to fend off the rain and was on the sideline during Tennessee's last drive down the field against Alabama.

"When it got down to the last down where Gary Wright was going to attempt the field goal, I ran down the sideline so that I was in a direct line with the ball and the goal post. I watched the kick and the ball sail toward the post. It couldn't have missed by more than the width or two of the football. It was that close. I remember the sadness and letdown after the miss."

Bobby was being recruited his senior year by many schools. In the Southeastern Conference, he made trips to Georgia and Alabama, in addition to Tennessee. He met Bear Bryant on his trip to Tuscaloosa and Vince Dooley at Georgia. They both had nice facilities, especially Alabama, and he knew the reputation of both coaches, but he also knew that he really wanted to go to Tennessee.

Vince Gibson, although the linebacker coach at Tennessee, had the recruiting responsibilities for Georgia, and from the results achieved, there is no doubt he did an excellent job. He sealed the deal with Bubba Wyche in 1964, and in 1966 did the little convincing that was necessary to bring another Georgia quarterback to Tennessee with Bobby Scott.

At Rossville High, Bobby followed a brother, Butch, who had also played quarterback. It was an athletic, hardworking, middle class family. His father worked at the Peerless Woolen Mills, then at a tannery in Chattanooga. His mother had more than she could do with keeping up with seven children and making banana pudding for Coach Gibson when he came down on recruiting trips.

Bobby started at quarterback as a sophomore in 1964 and continued the role during the next two years. His team won

Chris Cawood

twenty-nine and lost three during his career at Rossville.

Jimmy Weatherford played at arch-rival Dalton in 1964, and Bobby still kids him that Rossville never lost to Dalton when Bobby was the quarterback.

Rossville is just a long step across the state line from Chattanooga, so Bobby got up to Knoxville on several occasions to see the Vols in action.

Although he was in Georgia, the University of Georgia never entered seriously into his mind when he was being recruited. Two other players from Rossville had gone to Georgia and reported to Bobby that it wouldn't be the place for him to play.

Words of influence from close family friends in Chattanooga, including Judge Ray Brock, pointed him toward Tennessee. He visited Georgia, Alabama, Clemson, Georgia Tech, and Tennessee, before finally signing with the Vols.

On the freshman team in 1967, Bobby shared time at quarterback with Jim Maxwell. Bob Davis was the coach. They tied Vanderbilt at 14; beat Kentucky 27-20; lost to Georgia Tech 13-14; and lost to Alabama 3-7.

By 1968, Dewey Warren and Charlie Fulton had finished their eligibility, leaving Bubba Wyche and Bobby Scott as the two primary quarterbacks. Bubba was the senior and was going to play until he was hurt or until he showed that he couldn't handle the job. He didn't get hurt seriously that year, and he could handle the duties.

Bobby played in the backup role, often going into games after they had been decided. He was turning some heads and making a name for himself though in his appearances. Against Rice, he had two touchdowns passing and another running.

All in all, in 1968, he had four touchdowns passing to go with the one rushing. He threw the ball 55 times for 322 yards on 26 completions. By the time 1969 arrived, the quarterbacking job was his, and he was prepared to make the most of it.

111

Chattanooga made its last appearance on the Tennessee schedule as the first game in 1969. The team that had precipitated a near riot with their win over the Vols in 1958 was now no longer able to compete with the first class schools of the Southeastern Conference. It was a good warmup though for Scott to play a school that was almost in his home town. It was a blowout— Tennessee 31, Chattanooga 0.

Auburn, however, would be a test. Coach Doug Dickey's record was evenly matched with Shug Jordan since 1964. He had two wins, two losses, and a tie, the same as with Bear Bryant. But in 1969, Tennessee thrashed the Tigers 45 to 19 and made a strong statement that it would be a team to be reckoned with.

The next week in Memphis, the River City's Tigers also fell, 55 to 16.

In three games, the Vols were averaging almost 42 points to the opponents' 12.

"We had a great offensive team in 1969," Scott said in 1994, "but still the emphasis was on defense. If they can't score on you, they can't beat you."

In 1969, Tennessee probably had the best three linebackers in a group that it had ever had. Steve Kiner liked to bury opposing backs and then tell them they were dead. When Jack Reynolds plugged a hole, even Roto-Rooter couldn't remove him. Jackie Walker was the new kid. His quickness and movement to the ball would make him a big play maker.

The defensive backfield was solid for Tennessee. Senior captain Bill Young, a Knoxville South High School product who excelled on the basketball court and football field, was the safety. Mike Jones, who graced the cover of *Sports Illustrated* after the Alabama game in 1967, was at one corner. Smart, savvy, and quick Tim Priest was at the other.

Frank Yannosy and Steve Carroll anchored the defensive line.

Scott had an excellent group of backs and receivers. Gary

112

"High Pockets" Kreis was a senior with hands that attracted and kept the ball like flypaper. Lester McClain was a junior receiver with experience. Joe Thompson was a capable sophomore. Don McLeary played tailback but could catch the ball coming out of the backfield. Curt Watson from Crossville was developing into one of the best fullbacks that the Volunteer faithful had seen. Ken DeLong, a tested veteran, was still at tight end.

While it was possible to be distracted in the game before Alabama, Tennessee didn't let it happen in 1969. They wore out the Yellow Jackets of Georgia Tech 26 to 8 in Knoxville.

The Vols would be undefeated and untied going into Alabama week. That had not occurred since 1956.

In the rest of the world on the third week in October of 1969, various things were piquing the interest of those who followed science, politics, sports, and entertainment.

Dustin Hoffman was playing in "Midnight Cowboy."

During the just past summer, astronauts had walked on the moon, and Ted Kennedy had driven his car into Chappaquiddick Bay.

Billy Martin had just been fired after a stormy season as manager of the Minnesota Twins.

The New York Mets were finishing a miracle year in the World Series with Baltimore.

Across the way at Stokely Fieldhouse, Ray Mears and Stu Aberdeen were beginning practice with the Vol basketballers. Among the players would be Jimmy England, Robbie Croft, and Don Johnson.

Alabama had sustained a humiliating loss to lowly Vanderbilt the week before they were to meet the Vols. It was so bad that it was reported Bear Bryant moved into the dormitory with the players in preparation for their game with Tennessee.

Tennessee was ranked seventh in both the AP and UPI

polls. Alabama had fallen out of one and was ranked twentieth in the other. The Tide's record wasn't that bad. They had won three games—17 to 13 over Virginia Tech, 63 to 14 over Southern Mississippi, and 33 to 32 over Mississippi. But the 10 to 14 loss to Vanderbilt had fans talking in Tennessee and Alabama.

Among the reasons for the Bear being serious about the upcoming game were that he was going for his one hundredth victory at Alabama and the fact that he had never lost to any team two times in a row until Tennessee beat him for the second straight time in 1968. Three in a row would be too big a burden to bear. He was in his twenty-fifth year as a head coach.

In Knoxville, *News-Sentinel* sports editor Tom Siler wrote that "One question holds the key to the Tennessee-Alabama game Saturday: Can the Vol defense stop the passing of Scott Hunter and the running of Johnny Musso?"

Hunter was the junior quarterback who experienced the heartbreak of defeat the previous year in Knoxville. Musso was a hard-running sophomore who would be famous for his never-say-die style and bare midriff showing under a cut-off jersey. He would be playing in his home town of Birmingham.

Hunter would have pass targets in Pete Jilleba and George Ranager, among others.

Coach Dickey was not about to let up in his preparations for the Tide. He knew to take nothing for granted when it came to Alabama. The weather turned cold in Knoxville at midweek as he sent the Vols through some tough contact work.

Bobby Scott hadn't played in Birmingham before, so it was up to the "old" men on the team like Kiner, Reynolds, and Young to remind the younger ones "that you don't become a man until you beat Alabama in Birmingham."

Coach Dickey said on Thursday of Alabama week, "We're ready to go to Birmingham and play."

Captain Bill Young echoed the sentiment in Birmingham on Friday. "We came to play football." People began to get a hint of what was to follow.

Game day broke bright and clear in Birmingham. It would be a full house of over 72,000 to begin the festivities.

Some Big Orange supporters had hired a small plane to circle Legion Field with a banner claiming that area of Alabama as "Big Orange Country." Tide fans jeered and Vol fans applauded as the little plane flew its loops around the stadium.

Alabama won the toss and decided to receive. They were stopped on third down a yard short and had to punt.

Tennessee got the ball just 53 yards from Alabama's goal. Scott passed to Kreis for five. Don McLeary ran for nine, and Curt Watson plowed through the Tiders for fourteen to edge the ball down to the Bama five-yard line.

Scott looked for his sure-handed receiver again and found Kreis in the end zone. Kreis bobbled it before pulling it in for the first six points.

In recounting Kreis' exploits, Scott said his receiver "couldn't run out of sight in a month, but if you got the ball within his arm span, he was going to catch it. A great receiver to have."

So, Gary Kreis of Oliver Springs, Tennessee, did what every Tennessee boy dreamed of doing—he caught a touchdown pass against Alabama.

On Alabama's next series, the Tide went in reverse, thanks to Tennessee's Vic Dingus and James Woody. Alabama punted and then held Tennessee before getting the ball back.

Jackie Walker and Woody again stopped Musso, and Kiner cornered the quarterback for a loss of nine. Alabama had not moved beyond its 41-yard line on three possessions.

The Tide punted. Bobby Majors gathered it in at the Tennessee 29-yard line for the Vols. Majors, of the famous football family and another native Tennessean, did what every other Tennessee boy fantasized of doing—he returned the punt seventy-one yards for a touchdown. He was helped along with blocks by Priest, Young, and Ronnie Drummonds. George Hunt kicked the second extra point. Tennessee 14, Alabama 0.

"Everybody thinks I'm slow, so I ran as fast as I could. I tell you, there was some blocking on that play," Majors said later.

Scott remembers the punt return as he was preparing to reenter the game. Majors gave him another few minutes break with the touchdown. "Bobby had such a knack for seeing the field and knowing where the soft spots were. You just couldn't hit him. He wasn't fast, but he was quick. He had a fluid movement that you just couldn't get a good lick on."

Alabama was in deep trouble now. Disaster would strike with the next series. Neb Hayden relieved Hunter at quarterback. He pitched out poorly on a broken play and the ball bounced off Jerry Cash.

Linebacker Jackie Walker took the ball off Cash's shoulder pads and carried it back into the end zone twenty-seven yards away for Tennessee's third touchdown of the first quarter. Tennessee 21, Alabama 0.

In the second quarter, Alabama was finally able to penetrate midfield on its second possession. The Tide put together three first downs in a row until Kiner put a stop to such foolishness. he stormed in on a blitz and threw the relief quarterback Hayden for a fifteen-yard loss.

Scott moved the Vols down field, mixing runs of Watson and passes to Kreis with a keeper. Watson lost a fumble on the Tide four-yard line.

Hunter came back in to quarterback the Tide. They moved reasonably well down field on short passes and runs until Mike Jones intercepted at the Vol 35-yard line. Scott then hit on three passes to Kreis, McClain, and McClain to the five-yard line of Alabama. The Vols settled for a 22-yard field goal by Hunt to go in at halftime up 24 to 0.

In the third quarter, Alabama suffered no better at the hands of the Vols. Tim Priest picked off a Hunter pass. Then Kiner intercepted a pass at the Alabama 14-yard line. The Vols took another field goal from that. Benny Dalton snuffed out Alabama's last drive of the third quarter by recovering a fumble at the

Tennessee 31.

Scott drove Tennessee 69 yards in eleven plays with a nice run of his own and a thirty-one yard scamper by second-string tailback Bobby Patterson. Scott stepped into the end zone from two yards out on the first play of the fourth quarter.

It was Tennessee 34, Alabama 0, after the second play of the last quarter. Many Tide fans had suffered enough. Hundreds flocked to the gates to get an early start to prepare for Sunday prayer service.

Tennessee played everybody but the trainer they had brought on the trip and one player they decided to redshirt.

Alabama continued to struggle. When they threatened early in the quarter, Jones intercepted again.

Phil Pierce came in at quarterback for Tennessee and had an eighteen-yard run of his own. Tennessee kept it on the ground, trying to run the clock out, but scored again with a little over three minutes left.

Musso got two touchdowns in the last quarter for Alabama. Hayden and Hunter passed for 322 yards between them, but it didn't matter. They were doing all of the movement between the twenty-yard lines.

The one statistic that told the story of the day was that Alabama had only **TWENTY YARDS** rushing.

Tennessee played a complete game. The offense, defense, and special teams all accounted for touchdowns. The kickers kicked, and the punters punted.

Linebacker Steve Kiner had a career day. He sacked Tide quarterbacks five times. He had an interception, caused a fumble, and made eleven solo tackles.

It was no wonder that when Kiner caught up with the Bear after the game, Bryant shook his hand and said, "Son, you all have a fine team."

Tennessee did some things that no other team had ever done to Alabama or Bryant. The Vols had now won three in a row over Bryant's Alabama. It was the biggest margin by which any

Tennessee team had beaten Alabama. Tennessee scored as many points as had ever been scored against Alabama since 1907.

It could have been worse.

"This was the day Bobby Scott came of age as a bigtime quarterback. Bobby was cool, sure of himself, executed the option flawlessly, ran when he should and passed when he should pass. He didn't set any records. All he did was serve as the master engineer on a run that Tennessee and Alabama will not soon forget," wrote Tom Siler in the Sunday *News-Sentinel*.

"It was Bobby Scott's finest hour. The Tennessee quarterback has not perhaps been given the credit he deserves this season. Any team with a 5-0 record and an offensive productivity chart such as Tennessee has, has to have a fine QB. Against Alabama Scott was letter perfect, that's all. He threw beautifully, mixed his calls well, and you can't just write him off as a runner," seconded Ben Byrd in the Knoxville *Journal*.

Ed Harris of the Knoxville *Journal*, who two years earlier had written that Bear Bryant was in "the twilight of a championship coaching career," saw nothing in this game to change his opinion when he wrote, "Doug Dickey's Orange Shirts added new miseries to Paul (Bear) Bryant in the twilight of a great coaching career. It was Bryant's worst defeat by an SEC team."

Bryant wasn't taking it easy. "We'll lose all the faint-hearted now, but I'm not ready to give up, and I hope our team isn't either. You letter writers—to Hell with you. I don't have time to read your letters now or even to sort them. We've just got to get busy."

1969

	LINEUPS		SEASON RECORDS

	TENNESSEE	ALABAMA
LE	Kreis	Bailey
LT	Robinson	Ford
LG	Denbo	Ferguson
C	Bevans	Grammer
RG	Kell	Samples
RT	Balthrop	Wilder
RE	DeLong	Husband
QB	Scott	Hunter
HB	McLeary	Musso
HB	McClain	Jilleba
FB	Watson	Ranager

TENNESSEE

31	TN-Chattanooga	0
45	Auburn	19
55	Memphis State	16
26	GA Tech	8
41	Alabama	14
17	Georgia	3
29	S Carolina	14
0	Mississippi	38
31	Kentucky	26
40	Vanderbilt	27

GATOR BOWL

13	Florida	14

ALABAMA

17	VA Tech	13
63	Southern Miss.	14
33	Mississippi	32
10	Vanderbilt	14
14	Tennessee	41
38	Clemson	13
23	Miss. State	19
15	LSU	20
42	Miami	6
26	Auburn	49

LIBERTY BOWL

33	Colorado	47

GAME STATS	Tennessee	Alabama
First downs rushing	10	5
First downs passing	7	18
First downs by penalty	0	1
Total first downs	17	24
Attempts rushing	54	36
Net yards rushing	242	20
Passes attempted	18	47
Passes completed	9	32
Passes intercepted	0	5
Net yards passing	128	322
Total yards gained	370	342

Quarterback stats	Scott	Hunter	Hayden
Passes attempted	17	35	12
Passes completed	9	23	9
Passes intercepted	0	4	0
Net yards passing	128	221	101
Rushing attempts	7	3	8
Net yards rushing	26	-12	-51
Total yards	154	209	50

Vols–Scrubs, Too–Pack Tide in Big Orange Box

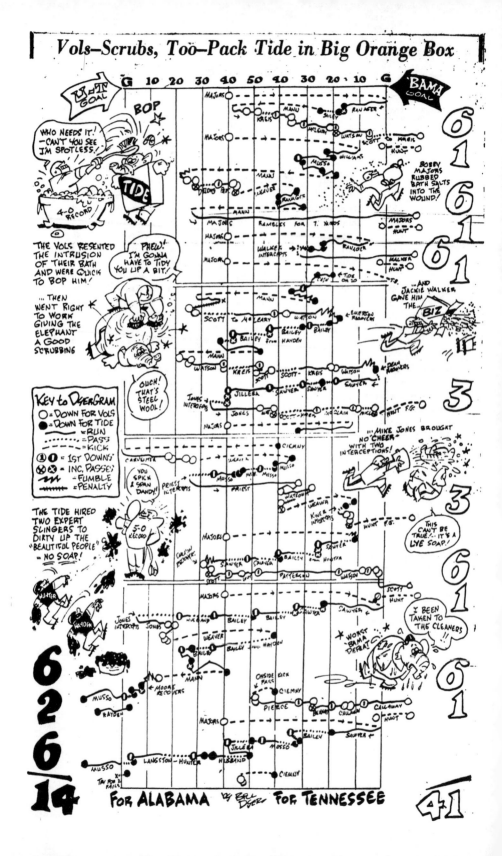

FOR ALABAMA by BILL DYER FOR TENNESSEE

1970—A Shutout

Bittersweet. That's a term that could have been applied to the remainder of the 1969 season.

After the walloping that the Vols had given to the Tide, nothing appeared to be able to stop them. They moved up in the polls with the Alabama massacre and subsequent wins over Georgia and South Carolina.

Only the November patsies of Mississippi, Kentucky, and Vanderbilt stood between them and a possible National Championship. Oops, don't say anything nasty about those folks in the Magnolia State. They don't take kindly to being called "mules." Ask Steve Kiner. Mississippi also happened to have a quarterback by the name of Archie, as in Archie Who?, Manning.

Tennessee played as though they had passed through New Orleans to be zombieized. Mississippi 38, Tennessee 0. Poof. How quickly those high aspirations disappeared on the field in Jackson.

Shortly after the last game of the season, rumors started circulating that Coach Doug Dickey might return to Florida, his alma mater, as head coach.

Dickey had fashioned a team at Tennessee that won nine of ten games and would play in the Gator Bowl against Florida on December 27.

His accomplishments were numerous since becoming head coach after the 1963 season. He had brought respect back to the program. The Vols were getting progressively better. They won the SEC Championship in 1967 and 1969.

In the rivalry with Alabama, Dickey had done more than hold his own. He had three wins over the Bear. The Bear had two over him. Who else in coaching could say they had a winning record against Alabama and Bryant?

It was true. Dickey left to return to Florida. Tennessee lost to Florida in the Gator Bowl 13 to 14.

What would have been the course of events if Dickey had stayed at Tennessee rather than leaving? Of course, it's pure speculation.

Bobby Scott has an idea. "I feel like if he had stayed here, he could have built on the great nucleus, the great tradition that he was building. There is no reason in the world why he couldn't have been like Bear Bryant was to Alabama. I think, deep down, he would tell you he made a mistake by leaving."

So much for speculation.

Tennessee, through its athletics board, president, and Athletic Director Bob Woodruff, decided to give the nod as new head coach to youthful assistant Bill Battle.

Battle had been an assistant since 1966. He was primarily the receivers' coach. He was five years younger than Doug Dickey had been when he began to rebuild Tennessee.

There were a few murmurs from distant corners of Tennessee about Battle being an Alabama graduate. He did not even have an indirect connection to Robert Neyland as Dickey had had through Coach Woodruff.

Of course, any questioning of Battle's desire to win for Tennessee was ridiculous. Anyone who had ever competed athletically, even in backyard croquet or badminton, knew that a competitive person wanted to win even if it meant defeating a child or spouse. In fact, there would probably be more pleasure in beating a former coach than in any other victory.

The players liked and respected Bill Battle. That has

Chris Cawood

increased over the years. Dewey Warren described Battle as being "a class act, a super nice guy."

"I really enjoyed playing under Coach Dickey and the staff that he had, but Coach Battle has a special place in my heart. He is a tremendous person," Bobby Scott said in 1994.

Scott believes that the players on the teams of 1969 and 1970 were very special. "When we put on the orange jersey on Saturday morning, it meant something. We were going out to do the job and to pay the price to win.

"Although I was from Georgia, we had a nucleus of Tennessee boys who ate and slept Tennessee football. We had kids like Tim Priest, Don Denbo, Mike Bevans, Joe Thompson, Curt Watson, Lester McClain, Phil Fulmer and others who were Tennessee boys. It was special."

The players and Coach Battle were anxious to get the season underway and prove they could carry on in the tradition they had learned. In 1970, they would get one extra chance since it was the first year that an eleventh game was added to the regular season schedule.

Southern Methodist came in as the opening game sacrificial lamb for the Volunteers. The feast was 28 to 3, Tennessee.

Auburn was into its second season as Tennessee's opening SEC opponent. The War Eagles spoiled the Vols opportunity to go undefeated into the Alabama game when they mugged Tennessee 36 to 23 in Birmingham.

A few doubters of Battle's ability appeared, but they were quickly silenced the next week when Tennessee drubbed Army 48 to 3 in Knoxville.

Georgia Tech would provide the opposition and tune-up for Tennessee preceding the Alabama game, as they had since 1966. Scott and the Vols put away the pesky Yellow Jackets 17 to 6 in Atlanta.

Except for Auburn, Tennessee had held its four opponents to an average of just four points per game.

Bryant's 1969 team at Alabama had produced more losses

123

(five) than any of his Tide teams since he became head coach in 1958. It was his second highest number of losses in his twenty-five years of being a head coach. He intended for things to change for the better in 1970.

However, an opening loss to Southern California in Birmingham by a whopping score of 21 to 42 did nothing to quieten the critics.

Alabama recovered with wins over Virginia Tech and Florida before losing to Mississippi in another shootout with Archie Manning, 23 to 48. The Tide thought they were getting well when they beat Vandy 35 to 11 the week before they were to play Tennessee.

Elsewhere during the third week of October in 1970, Baltimore was winning the World Series in five games over Cincinnati.

Winfield Dunn was running against John Jay Hooker for governor of Tennessee. Vice President Spiro Agnew said he was not grooming himself to run for President in 1976. President Richard Nixon and Billy Graham had shared Neyland Stadium in May of 1970, and some of the court cases resulting from protests were just being disposed of.

In Ohio, a special grand jury indicted twenty-five students while clearing members of the Ohio National Guard from any prosecution resulting from the deaths of students in a fateful incident there.

Joe Namath was starring with Ann Margret in "C. C. and Company" at the Capri Theater in Knoxville. George C. Scott was also starring in "Patton" at local theaters.

A little earlier in the year, Richard Nixon ventured out of the White House to wander among student protesters, accompanied in the early morning mist by just a valet and a few Secret Service men. He found some Syracuse University students who were on strike at school and protesting the Vietnam War in Washington.

124

"When we told him where we were from," one student recounted, "he talked about our football team."

It was to be the first meeting between Coach Battle and his former coach.

The Tide was battered and bruised going into the week of preparation against Tennessee. Alabama worked out in sweats on Tuesday because of nagging injuries to several players. Scott Hunter was among the walking wounded. He was held out of practice most of the week. Neb Hayden, who shared time at quarterback with Hunter in 1969's game, would start if Hunter was still hurt.

Johnny Musso had the second highest rushing average in the conference. He was averaging 5.6 yards per carry. Bryant wanted to get him the ball at least twenty times. He would be ready for Saturday. So would Tennessee's Curt Watson who was third in rushing in the conference.

Bobby Majors was first in the conference with five interceptions and second in the nation in interception return yardage.

"Alabama and Tennessee has always been THE game as far as I'm concerned," fullback Watson said. "If you don't know that when you arrive here, it takes only one year to find out. It's a great rivalry. . . just like dogs and cats. No matter what the records or score, I don't suppose there's ever been an easy Alabama-Tennessee game."

Both Tennessee and Alabama would have several players who were playing their first game in the series. On defense, Tennessee would have Bill Emendorfer, Frank Howell, Jamie Rotella, Conrad Graham, and David Allen getting their initial look at the Tide from across the line of scrimmage.

On July 4, 1970, a burglary occurred at the Roddy Manufacturing Building on Leslie Street in Knoxville. During Alabama week, it was finally disclosed what part of the valuable loot was that had been taken. An ad in the Knoxville *News-Sentinel* on Friday offered a $750 reward for the arrest of the people who had taken—twenty-one season tickets to Tennessee football games, most of them near the fifty-yard line.

Almost 65,000 waited in Neyland Stadium for the 2 p.m. kickoff to see if the impossible could be done—four in a row over Alabama. It was clear and nippy when Alabama and Tennessee put their players on the field to begin the battle.

Tennessee took the kick but couldn't move. Bobby Majors punted, and Alabama returned the favor, kicking after three tries. Tennessee managed a first down but punted again just a series later.

Captain Tim Priest started the thieving festivities by picking off Neb Hayden on a deflected pass and running it back to the Tide sixteen-yard line.

Bobby Scott found Sonny Leach open and got the ball to the one. From there, Scott sneaked it in to give Tennessee a 7 to 0 lead after George Hunt kicked the extra point. The Tide was able to make three first downs on the next series behind Hayden's passing, but Jackie Walker and John Wagster made two good stops to force another punt.

After that, there was an exchange of six punts between Majors for Tennessee and Frank Mann for Alabama as the teams played for field position the last part of the first quarter and the first part of the second quarter. It appeared the teams had stacked their offensive guns in the dressing room and had forgotten to bring them out to the ball field.

Musso got a few yards but paid dearly for every inch of ground with Emendorfer, Howell, and John Wagster filling the gaps, and Walker, Rotella, and Graham finishing him off. Alabama decided if they couldn't go through the linebackers, they would try going over. Another mistake. Rotella intercepted a Scott Hunter pass at the Vol 30.

Tennessee punted again after failing to move the ball. Alabama, trying to even it up before halftime, had Hunter moving the ball through the air to David Bailey. When they tried it again, Walker grabbed Tennessee's third interception of the day.

Bobby Scott passed long, but Alabama intercepted as time expired in the first half. Tennessee 7, Alabama 0. To the veteran observers, it looked like another old-fashioned defensive slobber-knocker.

Hunter had thrown two interceptions and Hayden had thrown one for the Tide in the first half. Bryant, always wanting to be an equal opportunity coach, sent Hayden back in on the first series of the second half. On his first pass, he was promptly intercepted by Graham. Tennessee had spread the thievery around with two made by linebackers, one by a safety, and one by a cornerback.

After Graham returned the interception fifteen yards to the Alabama 43, Tennessee was able to put together a decent drive. Scott made two clutch passes to Joe Thompson to keep the drive alive. Curt Watson plowed forward for a thirteen-yard gain, throwing a shoe in the deal, and took the ball to the Tide 18.

A loss on second down made it third and eleven. Scott once again hooked up with Thompson who lugged the ball down to the four. Don McLeary made it 13 to 0 with a four-yard run, following a vicious block by Watson on the corner. Hunt's kick gave the Vols a fourteen point cushion with under eleven minutes left in the third.

Alabama wasn't dead. Bear's boys drove fifty-four yards before stalling. The attempted thirty-eight yard field goal failed.

The Vols got a first down on the next series before Scott threw his second interception to Steve Higginbotham, tying for most receptions of Scott passes for the day.

Hunter returned the favor on Alabama's series, throwing the ball in Priest's territory. He returned it to the Alabama 20 before a clipping penalty set the Vols back. Nothing came of the threat.

Alabama didn't punt the entire second half. They didn't have to. Tennessee was picking the ball out of the air before they had the chance. Hunter had three interceptions to Hayden's two, nearing the end of the third quarter.

Bama drove to the Tennessee 43 before Hunter threw his fourth interception. Bobby Majors took this one on a high stretch and weaved his way seventeen yards down the field. Behind the running of Watson and Steve Wold, Tennessee squeezed a thirty-five yard field goal, making it 17 to 0 with just twelve minutes left in the game.

Hayden came back in for the Tide after the kickoff. On first down, Hayden threw to his right end who was met by Tennessee's right cornerback David Allen. The ball popped up and was grabbed by Jackie Walker. He rambled twenty-two yards for the touchdown. It was his second one against Alabama off of interceptions.

"All I could see was the red flag in the corner," Walker related of his run for the score. Tennessee 24, Alabama 0.

That was that. Except Alabama kept throwing. They had no choice, down by twenty-four in the fourth quarter.

Priest got his third interception off Hunter to tie a school record, shared by Albert Dorsey and Bill Young.

Alabama's deepest drive was to the Volunteer 18 late in the game. There Howell snuffed out the threat with a fumble recovery.

Bryant and his student, Coach Bill Battle, met at midfield after the game. Battle doesn't remember what was said. He was too excited with his first win over his old coach.

While the point difference wasn't as great as in 1969, Tennessee did something to the Tide that had not been done in eleven years—they held Alabama scoreless. Never before had the Vols shut out an Alabama team coached by Bryant. They would never again.

In 1970, the 24 to 0 triumph of Coach Battle, Quarterback Bobby Scott, Buddy Bennett's Bandits, and the whole team evened the series at twenty-three wins each. That was the last time that the teams have been even in the series.

The eight interceptions by Priest, Rotella, Majors, Walker, and Graham were a record. The five against Scott Hunter were the most against a Tide quarterback, except for the five against Kenny Stabler by Tennessee in 1967. Priest was named national defensive back of the week.

The defensive backs of this era (Priest, Mike Jones, Conrad Graham, Bill Young, and Bobby Majors) still sit at the top of the list in pass interceptions twenty-five or so years later. During the whole season of 1970, the defense took thirty-five interceptions, which is also still tops.

In the 1970 Alabama game, Curt Watson outran Johnny Musso, 91 to 68, on eight fewer carries.

Bobby Scott only had 55 yards passing and completed six of nineteen. But that was all that was needed. The defense did the rest.

"We just took over for each other. If something went wrong, if I threw an interception, or if we fumbled, we knew the defense would come in there and shut them down. By the same token, if the defense had a break down, they knew the offense could score some points. We had confidence in each other," Bobby Scott explained about the 1970 Tennessee team.

The week following Alabama, Florida came to Neyland Stadium led by Coach Doug Dickey. Fans and players looked forward to the meeting with the coach who had rebuilt Tennessee. The Vols won 38 to 7.

With ten wins against one loss in the regular season, Tennessee went to the Sugar Bowl and beat Air Force 34 to 13. It was a good first season for the young coach.

Bobby Scott's eligibility ended after the 1970 season. What would Tennessee's team have been like in 1971 if Scott had still been there? What if a year of eligibility had not been squandered in 1968 when he was a back-up to Bubba Wyche and played in a clean-up role?

In 1994, Bill Battle was asked that question.

"I really believe we would have won the National Championship. We had a great defensive team. We didn't have an experienced quarterback. We went through four quarterbacks."

Bobby Scott has often pondered the same question. "If I'd been redshirted in 1968 and been able to play that '71 season, it would have been interesting to see what would have happened. I'd like to have had a shot at it. I really would."

Instead, Bobby went on to twelve years of backing up Archie Manning with the New Orleans Saints.

Coach Bill Battle's following Tennessee teams were unable to defeat Alabama. He lost six straight before being forced out to make way for a Tennessee product who people thought would restore the series to a dignified rivalry.

Bear Bryant was so disgusted with the four straight losses to Tennessee and his team's second straight season of losing five games that he totally retooled the offense.

It could never be said that Bryant was altogether in favor of passing the ball forty or fifty times again. He wasn't. He went to the wishbone offense and won eight SEC titles over the next nine years.

Someone asked him before the 1971 Tennessee game if there would be eight interceptions by the Vols that year. "No. We won't throw the ball eight times this year," he said.

Bobby Scott made the adjustment from starter to backup quite well. He understood the hierarchy. He was drafted in the fourteenth round, Archie Manning in the first. "He and I worked together on the sideline, trying to put together things that would work for our offense. Archie's a tremendous person. I feel good about being able to be a friend of his."

Bobby finished out his pro career with the New Jersey Generals in 1983.

At Tennessee, Scott was "just an outstanding leader," according to Phil Fulmer who played guard on the offensive line when Scott was quarterback. "After our game preparation meetings, Bobby would get up and basically go through the entire game plan. It was almost like he memorized it. It was very impressive. Bobby was a very intelligent player."

"I thought Bobby had the strongest arm I had ever been associated with at Arkansas or Tennessee up to that point. He could throw the ball deep really well," Doug Dickey remembered in 1994.

Bill Battle saw Scott as "an excellent passer with really quick feet."

Scott lives in the Farragut area of Knox County now. He is a sales representative for Balfour, watches a lot of Tennessee football, and shares the microphone with Tim Priest on a call-in radio show after Vol games.

His son, Benson, is a senior quarterback at Farragut High who has all A's except for one B. Taylor, his daughter, is nine and a cheerleader for the little league teams. Bobby and his wife Pat recently celebrated their twentieth wedding anniversary.

"A quarterback is gauged on wins and losses," he said, speaking of other Tennessee players. But for Bobby Scott, it is written: TWO WINS, NO LOSSES ON THE THIRD SATURDAY IN OCTOBER.

CAREER STATS OF BOBBY SCOTT

	RUSHING		PASSING			
	CARRIES	YARDS	ATTEMPTS	COMPLETIONS	YARDS	TD'S
1968	32	-3	55	26	322	4
1969	90	123	191	92	1352	14
1970	51	89	252	118	1697	14
TOTALS	173	209	498	236	3371	32

1970

LINEUPS

	TENNESSEE	ALABAMA
LE	Thompson	Bailey
LT	Robinson	Rosser
LG	Fulmer	Hand
C	Bevans	Raines
RG	Kell	Drinkard
RT	Balthrop	Hannah
RE	Young	Moore
QB	Scott	Hayden
TB	McLeary	Musso
WB	Trott	Cash
FB	Watson	Brungard

SEASON RECORDS

TENNESSEE

28	S Methodist	3
23	Auburn	36
48	ARMY	3
17	GA Tech	6
24	Alabama	0
38	Florida	7
41	Wake Forrest	7
20	S Carolina	18
45	Kentucky	0
24	Vanderbilt	6
28	UCLA	17
SUGAR BOWL		
34	Air Force	13

ALABAMA

21	Southern Cal	42
51	VA Tech	18
46	Florida	15
23	Mississippi	48
35	Vanderbilt	11
0	Tennessee	24
30	Houston	21
35	Mississippi St	6
9	LSU	14
32	Miami	8
28	Auburn	33
ASTRO-BLUEBONNET BOWL		
24	Oklahoma	24

GAME STATS	Tennessee	Alabama
First downs rushing	8	11
First downs passing	4	13
First downs by penalty	0	1
Total first downs	12	25
Attempts rushing	41	38
Net yards rushing	153	87
Passes attempted	21	51
Passas completed	7	26
Passes intercepted	2	8
Net yards passing	60	271
Total yards gained	213	358

Quarterback stats	Scott	Hayden	Hunter
Passes attempted	19	26	25
Passes completed	6	14	12
Passes intercepted	2	3	5
Net yards passing	55	163	108
Rushing attempts	4	6	--
Net yards rushing	11	-16	--
Total yards	66	147	108

Tide's Hunter Is No Match for Vol Pigskin Hunters

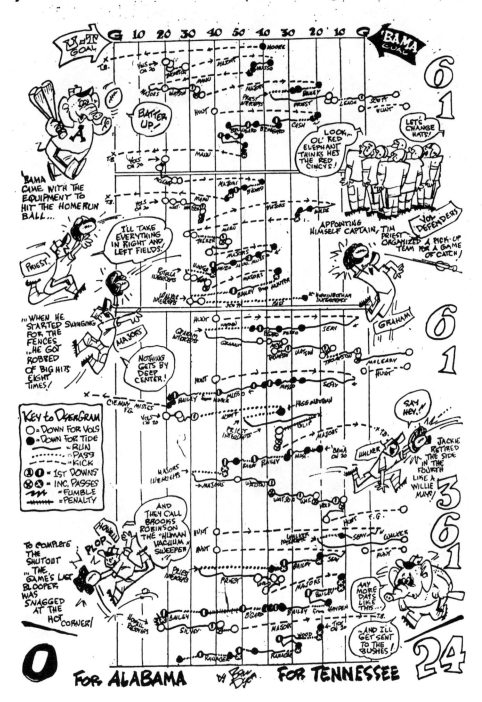

Bobby Scott still has the steady eyes of a quarterback who led the Vols over Alabama twice.

Bill Battle

When twenty-eight-year-old William E. Battle assumed the reins of the Tennessee football program in 1970, he began at a hectic pace. Now, he can sit back behind a large desk in a very nice office complex outside north Atlanta and reflect on those years.

Doug Dickey had rebuilt the program to a point that success was expected. After a SEC championship in 1969, could a national championship be far away?

Perhaps it was those expectations that finally did Bill Battle in as a coach. The expectations had to be met not only by on-the-field coaching—which Battle greatly enjoyed—but by recruiting and keeping the players eligible academically. Some schools and coaches were cutting corners in both categories. Battle wasn't going to do that.

Time was so precious. He hardly got to see his six-year-old Pat or two-year-old Mike during that first season.

He had been well prepared for coaching. He played under Bear Bryant at Alabama as a tight end in 1961, 1962, and 1963. He was good enough to be named to the All 1960's team at his position.

Before coming to Tennessee as a receivers' coach in 1966, he had already coached at West Point and a couple of other stints with notable coaches. He had watched the development of Warren,

Fulton, Wyche, and Scott as quarterbacks before he coached his first game as the head man.

He has never looked back on his decision to get out of coaching after the 1976 season. He liked coaching. It was the other things that took away from it.

"The head coach really spends most of his time today doing things that aren't what you really like to do—which is to get out on the field and coach."

He sees good in the turn around of cheating in college athletic programs today. "It's now punished very severely. I think it's going in the right direction now."

Many things have changed with football from the time that Battle played in the sixties until the present. "There's no question that the black player changed college athletics in the South."

The other change was in the size of players. "Unlimited substitution, weight training, and dietary programs have made it possible to play young men who weigh 280, 290, or 300 pounds."

Battle played at 190 to 210 pounds. He remembers that Coach Bryant delighted in taking fullbacks and turning them into linemen. "There was no weight program. We didn't even lift weights."

What about his record at Tennessee against Alabama?

"I don't think there is any question about it. Wherever you are, you have to beat your biggest rival in a certain amount of time or you aren't going to be around. If I lose six, or Johnny loses seven in a row, or if Tennessee beats Alabama seven times in a row, I promise you, they aren't going to have the same coach there. That's life in the big city."

Battle is trim and fit for a man in his early fifties. He appears to be enjoying life and his business. And why not? He has a family business that those two sons, Pat and Mike, help run. Their wives help when they aren't having babies. Bill's wife, Eugenia, has helped build the business. Their daughter, Shannon, who is nineteen has also contributed.

What is the business?

Well, Bill Battle hasn't left college athletics altogether. He runs one of the biggest, if not the biggest, licensing operation in the country.

Every T-Shirt that says Tennessee and is orange, every license plate, jogging suit, ball cap, coffee mug, cushion seat, or whatever else the imagination allows to be created that trades on the name, color, or reputation of the University of Tennessee or its athletic department, is supposed to be licensed. The university gets its cut. Battle is the one who sees to it that it's done.

He has a staff of forty-five which includes three lawyers, two CPA's, three auditors, a marketing staff, and administrative staff. The operation takes up twelve thousand square feet of the office building.

At present, Collegiate Concepts or Collegiate Licensing Company represents 140 colleges and universities, bowl games, and conferences. Another of his licensing companies, Battle Enterprises, does the same business for NASCAR. Tennessee is among the top ten universities in revenue produced by licensing. Since starting the business, Battle's company has paid over a $100 million to colleges and universities in fees collected for them.

He can do all this, have his family near him, and not worry about disgruntled sports fans writing letters to the local newspapers.

Last year Battle's company helped the University of Tennessee earn nearly a million dollars.

Bill Battle after winning the Sugar Bowl in 1971 (above) and at his licensing business near Atlanta in 1994 (below).

Rocky Top

Whether it was coincidence, serendipity, or whatever—the song that would later become the unofficial Volunteer spirit song was being composed in Gatlinburg during the same month that the Big Orange was beating Alabama in 1967.

Boudleaux and Felice Bryant were holed up in Room 388 at the Gatlinburg Inn, working practically non-stop on a collection of songs for Archie Campbell, Bob Ferguson, and Chet Atkins about the golden years of life. They weren't new to the song writing business. Among their hits were "Wake Up Little Susie," "Bye Bye Love," and "Love Hurts." Among the other artists they had written for were The Everly Brothers, Little Jimmy Dickens, Bobby Bare, and The Osborne Brothers.

They had traveled to Gatlinburg and the mountains every year since 1952 to get away for intense writing sessions. By 1967, they had become regulars back stage at the Grand Ole Opry.

After laboring so long and hard on the project, Felice cried out to do something different as a diversion.

Boudleaux didn't want to be distracted from the project. He resisted Felice's entreaty at first, but he then gave in, taking up his guitar and strumming hard on the strings. "How's this?" Felice remembers her husband asking. "Rocky Top you'll always be, home sweet home to me. . . ."

Felice added lines as they both got into the spirit of the

little ditty. "He accepted every dumb line I said, just to get it over with. About ten minutes later it was finished."

They put it away and went back to their real work. A few weeks later, Sonny Osborne asked them if they had any new tunes that might be suitable for the brothers. Sonny took it after hearing about four measures of the song. The rest is history.

W. J. Julian became band director at Tennessee in 1961. He instituted the circle drill, collaborated on the T that the team runs through as the players come onto the field, and brought in "Rocky Top."

Most appropriately, "Rocky Top" was first played by the Pride of the Southland Band in 1972 at the Alabama game.

"We just sorta used it in a drill, and the fans loved it so much that it became a fight song. It's a contagious tune. I don't know how many times per game it's played now," Dr. Julian said in 1994. He retired as band director in 1993.

Now, the song is played every place Tennessee travels. Many musicians at bars and restaurants where Tennessee has played in bowl games have had to do a quick study on the tune. At Tennessee's last appearance in the Sugar Bowl in 1991, "Rocky Top," played by a large black gentleman on a bass horn at the head of Bourbon Street, serenaded Vol fans returning after the come from behind victory over Virginia.

It has been played many places on a variety of instruments. However and wherever, it gets the orange blood flowing. For those uninitiated, here are the lyrics:

Rocky Top

By Boudleaux and Felice Bryant

Wish that I was on ol' Rocky Top
Down in the Tennessee hills
Ain't no smoggy smoke on Rocky Top
Aint' no telephone bills

140

Chris Cawood

Once I had a girl on Rocky Top
Half bear, other half cat
Wild as a mink, but sweet as soda pop
I still dream about that

Chorus

Rocky Top you'll always be
Home sweet home to me
Good ol' Rocky Top
Rocky Top Tennessee, Rocky TopTennessee

Verse II

Once two strangers climbed ol' Rocky Top
Lookin' for a moonshine still
Strangers ain't come down from Rocky Top
Reckon they never will
Corn won't grow at all on Rocky Top
Dirt's too rocky by far
That's why all the folks on Rocky Top
Get their corn from a jar

(Repeat chorus)

VerseIII

I've had years of cramped-up city life
Trapped like a duck in a pen
All I know is it's a pity life
Can't be simple again

(Repeat chorus)

Johnny Majors at Tennessee (above) and Pittsburgh (below).

Johnny Majors

The Majors family was definitely football oriented. Father Shirley Majors coached at Moore County High for six years, at Huntland for eight, and for twenty-one at the University of the South at Sewanee.

Johnny's brothers, Bill and Bobby, played after him at the University of Tennessee. Brother Joe quarterbacked at Florida State, while Larry played for Shirley at Sewanee. Sister Shirley Ann was a cheerleader at U-T.

Shirley won the Football Writers Association small college coach of the year in 1973 while Johnny was winning the same award in Division I.

Bill was killed in that tragic accident on October 18, 1965, that took three coaches' lives. Shirley didn't live to see Johnny defeat Alabama as a coach, dying on April 5, 1981.

During his playing career at U-T, Johnny established passing records from his tailback position that would last until the Swamp Rat came along. He was the runner-up in Heisman voting. In his senior year in 1956, Majors led Tennessee to an undefeated regular season under coach Bowden Wyatt.

Majors became a head coach at Iowa State in 1968 after years of being an assistant. In 1973, he moved to Pitt. He coached and Tony Dorsett ran as Pitt won the National Championship in 1976. He was again named national coach of the year.

It was natural for Tennessee to look to Majors when it was

decided that Bill Battle's time was over. He was a local man, a former star player, a Heisman runner-up, and now a nationally recognized coach with—A National Championship. That was what fans coveted more than anything.

Some fans began to make reservations for the French Quarter as soon as Majors was hired. Gumbo and crawfish recipes began appearing in local papers.

Majors tried to downplay the enthusiasm in as far as fans expectations were unreasonably high. However, he knew the fans and the administration did expect results. Among the results they expected were wins over arch rival Alabama. It had been six years since Tennessee had defeated Alabama when Majors took over. The fans wouldn't wait six more.

He managed only one winning season out of his first four, but after that he had only one other losing season. However, in his first four seasons, Tennessee only got as close as ten points to Alabama. Alabama's wishbone was running roughshod over the Tennessee defense, while Tennessee's offense was averaging a measley eleven points against the Tide defense.

Over the next two seasons, U-T's coaches would recruit two very talented quarterbacks and keep another one who was a savvy student of the game.

In the early and mid-sixties, Tennessee had dipped into Georgia to pluck three fine quarterback prospects in Dewey Warren, Bubba Wyche, and Bobby Scott. Where would they go to find another who could just say NO to Alabama?

1982-Alan Cockrell

If Norman Rockwell had still been alive and doing the covers for the *Saturday Evening Post* in February 1981, he would have had the perfect embodiment of sports recruiting Americana at Alan Cockrell's high school gymnasium in Joplin, Missouri, on a cold basketball game night.

At the time, Cockrell's services were wanted by many colleges. The Big Eight, the SEC, and the Southwest Conference would all be represented before the night was over. The next day was national signing day. Football season was over, and Alan was playing his normal basketball game on Tuesday night at Parkwood High School.

He had already signed to play football with the Oklahoma State Cowboys. But that letter of intent, at the time, was not binding until the national letter was signed, which couldn't be done until the following day. Cockrell was still open game for the other schools, conferences, and coaches.

Jimmy Johnson, later to coach the University of Miami and the Dallas Cowboys, was the coach of Oklahoma State. Dave Wannstedt, presently the head coach of the Chicago Bears, was, in 1981, Johnson's assistant. Johnny Majors was head coach at Tennessee, and Doug Mathews was an offensive assistant. Lou Holtz was the head coach at Arkansas.

At a time out in the basketball game, Alan was walking to the sideline when he looked up and gathered in the scene fit for a Rockwell masterpiece.

His parents were sitting in the stands enjoying the game. By his mother's side sat Johnny Majors and Doug Mathews. By his father's side, sat Jimmy Johnson and Dave Wannstedt. Each of the coaches was duly solicitous of Alan's parents' views and concerns.

Alan played out the game, sneaked out the back door, and drove with a friend over the state line to Kansas to spend the night at his buddy's house. He didn't want to deal with all the coaches again. He had his mind made up.

"About ten-thirty that night, I get a call from Lou Holtz. And I start thinking to myself, 'How in the heck did he know where I was?' About two days later, I put it all together. My mom was a huge Lou Holtz fan. Arkansas was only about an hour and a half from Joplin. She had told him where I was."

How did this young man come to be wanted by so many illustrious coaches? And why did he say **YES** to Tennessee and **NO** to Jimmy Johnson, Lou Holtz, and Bear Bryant, among others?

Alan grew up in Galena, Kansas, which sits in the southeast corner of the state just across the line from Joplin, Missouri, and a few miles from the Oklahoma border. Both his parents were in education—his mother an English teacher and his father an administrator.

They had a 150-acre farm where some beef cattle grazed, but it was more of a hobby for his father than a business. His brother was twelve years older and his sister ten years older than Alan. Instead of competing with them, he got into organized ball from an early age. Again, the season determined the shape and texture of the ball that he held in his hand

Like Bubba Wyche before him, Alan traveled around to the surrounding states playing on baseball and basketball teams that

146

saw a lot of action. Sometimes they would play forty games a season in basketball and probably more in baseball when he was twelve years old.

His football skills were not neglected as a youngster. On November 3, 1974, he won the eleven-year-old division of the Punt, Pass, and Kick contest at Arrowhead Stadium when the Kansas City Chiefs played the New York Giants. He went on to compete in the regional contest in Pittsburgh in December of that year.

At Riverton Junior High, near Galena, Alan's eighth grade team did not lose a game in football—or basketball—or any track meet. By the ninth grade, he was starting on the high school football team. It was a very small school.

Joplin, Missouri, lay just across the state line. Alan had played ball with many of the boys who were going to Parkwood High School in Joplin. It was a school of fifteen hundred or so students. Both his mother and father wanted him to go there to finish high school. There would be more competition athletically and a better curriculum academically.

Alan made the transition from very small high school to very large high school in stride. By that time, he was pushing at six feet in height and weighed about 170. As a sophomore, he started at quarterback on the football team, at guard on the basketball team, and at the center fielder position in baseball.

At the end of his junior year, he began to get letters from colleges that were interested in his athletic talents. All of the Big Eight schools wrote him, along with a half dozen from the Southwestern Conference and Vanderbilt out of the Southeastern Conference.

He had versatile football abilities left over from his Punt, Pass, and Kick days. He was the quarterback, the punter, and the kicker. His longest punt was 65 yards, and he had a 47-yard field goal to his credit. He made first team All-State as a kicker and punter and second team as a quarterback his junior year.

His senior season brought even more recognition as

147

Parkwood won the state championship, going 14 and 0. Alan was named to the High School Coaches Association Prep All-American team at quarterback.

By the end of his senior season, over a hundred schools were in hot pursuit of the dark-haired schoolboy phenom from Joplin, Missouri. Some of the names on the list were Notre Dame, UCLA, USC, Texas, Arkansas, Alabama, and Tennessee. He didn't fit into the offensive scheme of Oklahoma as well as he did of Oklahoma State. There was always the pressure by local fans to stay with a local school. He also wanted to be close enough that his parents could see him play.

He signed with Oklahoma State and Coach Jimmy Johnson, who appeared to be going places.

Word spread around town. But most of the townspeople had heard it wrong. Every place Alan went, people would come up and congratulate him on signing with the Sooners. When he told them he was going to be an Oklahoma State Cowboy and not an Oklahoma Sooner, he learned quickly that most everyone in town considered the Cowboys a step down from the Sooners.

He started re-thinking the situation. "I just didn't want to play second fiddle to Oklahoma my entire college career."

The more he pondered it, the more Tennessee kept coming back to mind. The Volunteer program fit the criteria that he demanded.

Of the hundred schools who sought his services, Tennessee was among about ten who agreed to let Alan play baseball his freshman year. The others, including Alabama, had told him he could play his second year, but he'd have to be in spring practice his freshman year. His reply to all those schools and coaches, including Bear Bryant, was, "I don't want to visit then."

Tennessee had years ago wedded the brawn of football with the speed of track. The coaches there were not reluctant to allow a talented young man to display all his athletic ability if he wanted.

Until his official visit to U-T, Alan had never even passed through the state, although he may have flown over a time or two.

148

He knew little about the Tennessee-Alabama rivalry and couldn't whistle "Rocky Top" from memory. Of course, there was little reason for him to know of any *rivalry* since he was just seven-years-old the last time the Vols had prevailed against the Tide. What rivalry?

Although the other Big Eight schools had to honor the league letter signed by Cockrell, no school outside the conference was so obligated until he signed the national letter of intent.

What else tilted Cockrell toward Tennessee?

"That stadium was incredible. I had a great time on my visit down there. Bill Bates took me out on my recruiting trip, and I had a good time." The only drawback was that it was a little farther from home than he wanted to go. The other features overrode that one hindrance.

"I called Coach Mathews, and I said, 'Coach Mathews, I want to come to Tennessee.'"

So, that's how Johnny Majors, Doug Mathews, Jimmy Johnson, and Dave Wannstedt ended up in Joplin, Missouri, on a cold February night in 1981. Lou Holtz wasn't far behind. A mother was supplying him with her son's phone number at his hideaway.

When Alan Cockrell arrived for pre-season practice in August 1981, he asked for the same jersey number he had worn in high school—Number 11. It wasn't available. Daryl Dickey already had it. Cockrell settled for Number 6.

Freshmen were now eligible. As it would turn out, Alan would get his baptism under fire in short order.

Johnny Majors, in 1981, was into his fifth year of a four year "rebuilding" program, as some disgruntled fans referred to it. One of the reasons that Majors was brought in was the expectation that a native Tennessean, an All-American as a player, and a runnerup for the Heisman Trophy could quickly restore respectability. Respectability meant beating Alabama and climbing into the top echelon of the Southeastern Conference. Bill Battle had been canned after losing to the Tide six times in a row. Majors had now lost four in a row by an average score of 11 to 27.

The year did not begin on a promising note. The Vols were humiliated at Athens by Georgia. The score was 0 to 44. Sure, the Bulldogs had Herschel Walker. But how could the coaches account for Tennessee's lack of offense?

Maybe the following week would be the answer. Not hardly. Southern Cal trounced Tennessee in Los Angeles 43 to 7.

Tennessee's lone touchdown came on a pass from freshman Alan Cockrell to Randall Morris. Up to that point, the coaches had stayed with their older quarterbacks.

Over the weekend, Alan dropped by where the following week's depth charts were listed. They showed the players and press where each player ranked at that time in order of starting, being second-string, or third-string. To his surprise, Alan had moved up to the first slot in the quarterback position.

He was so excited he called his father to tell him the good news. His father was silent for only a second when Alan told him he would be starting the next week. "Well, Alan, hell, I guess they figure if they were losing with two senior quarterbacks, they might as well lose with a freshman."

Whatever it was, Alan Cockrell started the first home game of the season the following week against Colorado State and led the Volunteers to a much needed 42 to 0 victory. The freshman had come through. Tennessee was back, and Alabama was just four weeks away.

But first there would be Auburn. Tennessee took the opening kickoff and moved behind Cockrell's leadership to a first down. Then on the fifth play of the game, Alan Cockrell's season came to a painful conclusion. The anterior cruciate ligament in his left knee was torn when he planted his foot into the artificial turf and tried to make a cut while taking a blow that rolled him over. It was no cheap hit. It was just a terrible injury.

He didn't go to the 1981 Tennessee-Alabama game in

Birmingham. Instead he listened to bits and pieces of the game while he visited Gatlinburg. It wasn't much to listen to: Tennessee 19, Alabama 38.

Not only did the knee injury end his 1981 football season, but he also was unable to participate in baseball the next spring. So, the main reason he came to Tennessee—the opportunity to play football and baseball his freshman year—was taken from him by the injury.

"I was in a cast for twelve weeks and on crutches for sixteen," Alan remembers. "I had a total reconstruction of my knee. They just cut the torn parts out, sewed it back together, and stapled it to my knee."

By the opening of the 1982 season, Cockrell had struggled through a painful, vexing, and "character building" rehabilitation of his left knee. He would wear a brace for further protection.

Al Saunders had arrived as quarterbacks coach and helped to install a new, more efficient offense that would employ more drop back passing and fewer roll outs and options.

"Well, we've got world class sprinters at wide receiver. Why don't we throw it to them?" This was Saunders theory. They did and they did. Has Tennessee ever had a better and faster five receivers than Willie Gault, Mike Miller, Lenny Talyor, Darryal Wilson, and Clyde Duncan?

Even with these speedsters and Cockrell at quarterback, the Vols had their problems. On defense, they had a team that included Bill Bates, Mike Cofer, and Reggie White. However, Duke beat them on opening night by one, 24 to 25. U-T squeaked by Iowa State 23 to 21. Auburn won at Auburn 24 to 14. Back home, Tennessee only beat Washington State by a touchdown, 10 to 3. Certainly, this did not look like a team that would be able to stay with Alabama two weeks hence, especially with a trip to Baton Rouge and a date with the LSU Tigers sandwiched in between.

It would be the LSU game, though, that would give the Vols the confidence and impetus not only to face Alabama but to go on to other victories that year.

It was never anything to look forward to—going to crazy Tiger Stadium in Baton Rouge on a Saturday night. The fans were wilder than the caged tiger. Many teams' dreams had been shattered there in bayou country before.

When Tennessee managed a 24-24 tie, the coaches saw improvement.

"I told the team we were playing an extremely tough team. If we didn't fight, we could get blown out of the ball park," Coach Majors told reporters after the game.

To Cockrell, though, "It was just a very empty feeling as I walked off the field." Cockrell, like all competitors, wanted nothing less than victory.

But it did show the Vols could stay with a tough team on the road. Perhaps the offense and defense were gelling in time for Alabama week.

In October, 1982, Lamar Alexander was running for his second term as governor against Randy Tyree of Knoxville. Jim Sasser was facing Robin Beard. The 1982 World's Fair, a project pushed hard by Jake Butcher, wrapped around the campus area.

"An Officer and a Gentleman" was playing at the Kingston Cinemas in Knoxville, starring Richard Gere and Debra Winger. Knoxvillian David Keith was another of the prime actors. Liberace was sued for $113 million by a man in a "palimony" lawsuit.

The DOW Jones soared above the thousand level for the first time in 1982.

In other sports stories, the Milwaukee Brewers were playing the St. Louis Cardinals in the World Series. The NFL was on strike. The U-T trustees were considering a contract for architects to design a new $30 million basketball arena.

Alabama came into the week with a 5 and 0 record,

running through the schedule with their wishbone offense that was averaging 424 yards per game. The elusive Walter Lewis was the quarterback.

This would be Bear Bryant's last visit to Neyland Stadium. He had made many. As a player for Alabama, he played in 1935 the day after the team doctor took a cast off his broken leg. He had visited as a coach for Kentucky, but his greatest success had come as the Tide's coach. His record against the Vols at Alabama going into the 1982 game was 16-6-2.

"There was a time that I would get so worked up before our games with Tennessee that I had to pull over to the side of the road and vomit on the way to the office. I've overcome that now, but I still get a special feeling during the third week in October every year," Bryant said.

David Cutcliffe was a part-time coach for Tennessee in 1982. He had played for Alabama. He gave his perspective on the rivalry from the Alabama side: "There is some hatred involved in the Alabama-Auburn rivalry. That's not true in the Alabama-Tennessee series. This is a class football rivalry between two class football programs."

Two Tennessee graduates, Jim Goostree and Ken Donahue were on the Alabama staff. Donahue was assistant head coach, and Goostree was the trainer. "This is really their week as far as motivation," Cutcliffe continued. "Whenever Alabama beats Tennessee, Goostree and Donahue do a little dance in the dressing room. It's just sort of a little celebration in front of the players."

They had been dancing for eleven straight years. It was time to pick up their dance cards and pay the fiddler.

Alan Cockrell had little understanding of the special nature of the Tennessee-Alabama rivalry. He had never been to a game. He didn't grow up with it. While he was being recruited, both Alabama and Tennessee reminded him they were playing on

153

national television. Would he watch? He did—about a quarter's worth and turned it off. "Boring." It was raining and Tennessee was having a difficult time getting anything done. He was in Gatlinburg nursing his knee injury at the time of the 1981 game.

The first Alabama-Tennessee game he would see would be the one he started in 1982 as a nineteen-year-old sophomore.

The gravity of it dawned on him the day of the game.

"As soon as I woke up that Saturday morning, I opened up the sports page. There it asked: 'Will this be the twelfth year in a row? Will the Tide Roll over the Vols?' It actually didn't hit me to that point. This is serious. We need to beat these guys. I knew they were ranked Number Two in the country, undefeated, and had won five games that season.

"I flipped the page, and it had this big linebacker saying, 'I'm going to be hawking Cockrell all day long.' Then I'm like, this is getting personal now. That's when it really hit me.

"I began to understand the tradition at that point and how serious it was. It was serious, not only to the teams but to the fans.

"I remember we used to stay at a hotel out in west Knoxville before the game. When we took the buses to the stadium, we'd have police escorts. People just stopped on the sides of the road. You could just see the intensity in the eyes of the Tennessee fans.

"They were waving their orange and white shakers and yelling, 'Beat the hell out of those guys!' The fans would have loved to put on the uniform and go out and try to beat Alabama."

Bear Bryant had been coach at Alabama six years longer than Cockrell had been alive.

When Cockrell got onto the field, he knew the game would be everything he had read about and seen on the way to the stadium.

"We used to warm up a little early with the quarterbacks and kickers. Just throw and get warm until the visiting team came out and the remainder of our guys.

154

"I was watching as a huddle of reporters came out of the visitors' dressing room area. Then I noticed, it was Bear's hat. He was right there in the middle of all the reporters. He kind of walked out real slow, kind of mystical. The group of reporters broke up, and he just walked over to the goal post and leaned, leaned on the goal post, crossed his legs, folded his arms, and surveyed what was going on. I just stopped for about five minutes and watched him.

"The way he went onto the field was intimidating. There was an aura about his presence."

It was game time.

The Crimson Tide was a two-touchdown favorite and gunning for another national title.

Alabama took the opening kick-off, but Walter Lewis fumbled the first play when he faked too long to his fullback. The ball popped into the air and Mike Casteel recovered at the eleven-yard line. Tennessee couldn't push it in and settled for a 22-yard Fuad Reveiz field goal.

Just four minutes later, Jeremiah Castille intercepted a Cockrell pass, returning it to the Volunteer 19-yard line. Joe Carter later scored from the four.

"I remember their defensive backs being incredibly fast. In the first half of that game, I made Jeremiah Castille an All-American. He got three interceptions in the first half. Later, every time he made an All-American team, they showed him intercepting one of my passes," Cockrell said in 1994.

Alabama padded their lead with an 89-yard touchdown drive behind the running and passing of Lewis. The final play of that possession was a 35-yard pass to Jesse Bendross. Peter Kim kicked the extra point to make it 14 to 3 with about ten minutes to go in the half. It appeared to be another typical Alabama team that could strike quickly and was not deterred by giving up an early field goal.

Tennessee stalled on its next possession, but All-American punter Jimmy Colquitt punted a beautiful spiral 53 yards to Darryl White who fumbled. Five Tennessee players chased the ball to within inches of the goal line, but White came up with it.

Alabama couldn't move either.

Cockrell then found Willie Gault. Once Gault turned the burners on, all the defensive back could do was to read his jersey number quickly becoming fine print. It was good for 52-yards and a touchdown. The extra point made it 10 to 14, Alabama still leading.

Vince Clark intercepted a Lewis pass for Tennessee, and Reveiz kicked another field goal, making it 13 to 14 with 2:49 left in the half.

After Tennessee regained possession, Castille got his second Cockrell pass and took it to the U-T 42. Fans were praying for halftime and the playing of "Rocky Top," but Alabama had other ideas. Lewis hit Joey Jones for a 38-yard touchdown. Bear's boys were back up 21 to 13.

Not wanting to be stingy, Cockrell threw to Castille's side of the field again and regretted it. The half ended before Alabama could score.

Tennessee's coaches told the players at halftime that they had Alabama right where they wanted them—and they didn't mean in the locker room.

"Coach Saunders told me that we had the game plan set, and if I didn't throw the ball away, we could win," Cockrell recounted after the game.

Tennessee drove on the first possession of the second half down to the Tide's 28-yard line. Reveiz kicked his third field goal at 45 yards.

Just two plays later, Tennessee got the ball back on a fumble by Bama quarterback Ken Coley who was sharing the duties with Lewis. Cockrell found one of the other speedsters, Mike Miller, on a little hitch and go for a 39-yard touchdown. With the TD making the score 22 to 21 in the Vols favor, the coaches decided to go for two points to give them a field goal lead. Kenny Jones hauled in the football as though it was a gemstone. Tennessee 24, Alabama 21.

Reveiz wasn't through with the happiest day of his life yet. On the next possession of Tennessee, he booted his fourth three-pointer from forty yards. Tennessee 27, Alabama 21.

Tennessee's offensive line took over in the fourth quarter to dominate Alabama's defensive front. The names of DAVID JAMES, CURT SINGER, CHARLES GILLESPIE, MIKE FURNAS, BILL MAYO, STEVE KNIGHT, and JOHN MAT-THEWS should be written in capital letters for their contributions throughout the day and especially on the last touchdown drive of the day by Tennessee. A nine-play drive covered eighty yards. They were all runs. The tanks were moving them out.

Junior Chuck Coleman gained 139 yards on the day, 34 of them on a touchdown dash on the last drive.

Alabama players admitted it after the game. "I went against Curt Singer all day," one of them said. "He was something else. All of them. That guard (Mike Furnas) began to double me from the inside. They were blocking like nobody blocked us all year. And there wasn't any cheap talk and stuff."

Tennessee again went for two after the coaches got out their calculator and figured Alabama would then need two touchdowns and a combination of three extra points to beat them.

Although the score was 35 to 21 after Cockrell completed another two-point conversion to Kenny Jones, the Tide never quit. No one expected that they would.

Lewis led them down the field for a touchdown and extra point to make it 35 to 28.

After Tennessee ran a series and a little time off the clock. Alabama got the ball back on their forty with a minute and a half left in the game.

Cockrell remembers the sight, sounds, and feelings. "Walter Lewis was running all over the place. He ran the wishbone to perfection that day.

"When Mike Miller caught the pass for the touchdown, I remember how loud Neyland Stadium got at that point. People were just going nuts.

"With a minute and a half to go, it got deathly quiet. It was like the fans were remembering the last eleven years and were thinking 'How is Alabama going to pull it off this year?'

"You would think with 95,000 people there, they would want to make as much noise as possible to disrupt their offense. But they were deathly quiet, waiting for. . .something to happen."

Alabama did drive. Down near the end zone with just a paucity of seconds remaining, Lewis would get two chances.

He first went to old reliable Jesse Bendross. Tennessee defensive back Lee Jenkins made a spectacular dive barely knocking the ball away at the last second.

On what would be Alabama's final play, Lewis went to Joey Jones. Jenkins arrived at the same time as the ball, just before Bill Bates. The impact knocked the wind out of Jenkins, but better yet, knocked the ball loose and into the waiting hands of defensive end Mike Terry in the end zone. Seventeen seconds were left when Tennessee took over.

It was party time.

Of the 95,342 in attendance, all but about ten thousand were Big Orange berserk. The remainder were disappointed Tide fans.

The clock was counted down and the field stampeded. The chain link fence folded like wet cardboard. Police at first tried to protect the south end zone goal post after giving in to the crowd at the north end. But in this case, discretion was the better part of valor, and they retreated after the north goal post was hoisted as a battering ram against the south one.

Players couldn't get off the field. When they did, they came back for an encore. Cockrell wanted to speak to Coach Bryant but gave up on it. He made it to the dressing room that was empty and came back to find his teammates.

The band played "Rocky Top" and "The Tennessee Waltz" for as long as anyone wanted to listen. The party spread to the

Cumberland Avenue strip, from there throughout Tennessee, and to anyplace else where Tennessee alumni and fans heard the news.

The drought was over. In their last, as in their first meeting with the Bear as coach, Tennessee had won. Paul Bryant had enough wins in between to be satisfied. No, he wouldn't delay his retirement in order to get another shot at the Vols. "I'm glad to get away from here."

As for Johnny Majors, he remembers the game twelve years later as "one of the most exciting" he had been involved in. To go for "two points twice and make it" was an accomplishment.

"The game was important in that it broke the streak," he reflected.

Suddenly, eleven years of burden had been lifted from coaches, players, and fans. The Tennessee boys were especially happy. The ones from Lenoir City, Maryville, Memphis, Farragut, Chattanooga, Knoxville, Nashville and other towns across the state could now go home and tell the folks, "I played on a team that beat Alabama."

For a teenager from southeast Kansas who had come to Tennessee from Joplin, Missouri, the game was an eye opener. He may not have known much about the rivalry before he woke up on Saturday, October 16, 1982, but he sure got a dose of it before he went to bed that night.

Perhaps, also, the old saying was true that a Tennessee football player goes into his first Alabama game as a boy and comes out a man.

1982

GAME STATS	Tennessee	Alabama
First downs rushing	9	15
First downs passing	8	8
Total first downs	17	24
Attempts rushing	36	56
Yards gained rushing	177	318
Yards lost rushing	11	32
Net yards rushing	166	286
Passes attempted	29	22
Passes completed	18	10
Passes intercepted	3	2
Net yards passing	192	200
Total yards gained	358	486

Quarterback stats	Cockrell	Lewis
Passes attempted	29	22
Passes completed	18	10
Passes intercepted	3	2
Net yards passing	192	200
Rushing attempts	6	16
Net yards rushing	0	79
Total yards	192	339

TENNESSEE

24 Duke	25
23 Iowa State	21
14 Auburn	24
10 Washington St	3
24 Louisiana St	24
35 Alabama	28
21 GA Tech	31
29 Memphis State	3
30 Mississippi	17
28 Kentucky	7
21 Vanderbilt	28
PEACH BOWL	
22 Iowa	28

ALABAMA

45 GA Tech	7
42 Mississippi	14
24 Vanderbilt	21
34 Arkansas St	7
42 Penn St	21
28 Tennessee	35
21 Cincinnati	3
20 Miss. State	12
10 LSU	20
29 Southern Miss.	38
22 Auburn	23
LIBERTY BOWL	
21 Illinois	15

Food and Fun

Tennessee and Alabama fans plan other excursions during the third weekend in October. The centerpiece is the football game. But it is garnished on both ends by fun and frolic.

It is one of the best times of the year for the mountains. Alabama fans might come for the week and spend most of it in Gatlinburg. The chemical reaction in the leaves allows the golden glows of yellow and orange and the persistent crimson tones to paint the canvas of the mountains and valleys in hues that remind of the clash to come.

It is a time to relax, walk a few trails, and sit around a fireplace at night and talk about the games that have gone before.

Tennessee fans arrive from throughout the state and country for the most important game of the season. The armada of the Vol Navy arrives early and parties late. The captains and their mates can grill steak on board or take a leisurely walk along Neyland Drive by the river to Calhoun's On the River.

Calhoun's is famous for barbecue and a long wait on football weekends. It's usually worth it. Here again, fans can sit near the river as the sun sets, let the grease and juice from a slab of ribs drip down their wrists and reminisce about the great plays of days gone by.

For those with old money and good taste, the Regas Restaurant is at the end of Gay Street near the old railroad depot.

There customers are like family. One of the Regas family is likely to drop by the table, greet, and check on things himself. It has been there since before the memory of man.

For those of a more celebratory nature, there is Hoo-Ray's Sports Bar and Grill on Central near Jackson in what is called the Olde City. This is in the center of a restored area of Knoxville that hosts a variety of ethnic eateries and shops on a small scale of Savannah, Charleston, or New Orleans.

Hoo-Ray's has the appearance of Bourbon Street with the two-story building and wrought iron balcony railing. Inside, there is a bar, tables, an abundance of sports memorabilia, and usually a gathering of knowledgeable football minds on the third weekend in October and other times.

Hugh Ray Wilson, the proprietor, moves to a suite over-looking the real Bourbon Street in New Orleans anytime Tennessee makes it to the Sugar Bowl.

A unique place that serves Paducah style barbecue on the far west end of Knox county is Ott's. It is everything that Calhoun's, the Regas, and Hoo-Ray's are not.

Come early if you want some of Otto Melott's famous recipe barbecue. The small block building only has ten bar stools and three tables.

But people have stood in line for twenty-one years for Ott's pork and beef. Now run by his daughter, Carolyn Frost, Ott's opened in 1963 on Highway 70, known locally as Kingston Pike, at Dixie-Lee junction near Loudon County just two miles from the Watt Road Exit of I-40-75.

If a diner gets to Ott's early enough, he can walk around the inside wall and view a large array of schedules of every Tennessee season from 1963 to present with the score hand-written in after each game. The Kerns Bread style schedules now wrap all the way around the room to over the counter.

This is the year they want to write in another victorious score on the third Saturday in October.

1983—48 or Opposite

Georgia Tech burst Tennessee's bubble the game after Alabama in 1982 by whipping the Vols 31 to 21. The Big Orange went on to win three of their last regular season games which was good enough for a Peach Bowl bid. Iowa beat them in Atlanta 28 to 22.

The six win, five loss, and one tie season would have been considered mediocre except for the mid-season lift of beating the Tide.

Coach Johnny Majors was able to deflect criticism of his so-so record by pointing to a strong close to the regular season and optimism for 1983. Then they would have a seasoned quarterback, additional strong running backs, most of their receivers back, and an offensive line anchored by Bill Mayo, Curt Singer, and Glenn Streno. It was enough to say the defense would have Reggie White at tackle, not to mention Alvin Toles, Carl Zander, Reggie McKenzie, and Dale Jones in the linebacker corps.

Despite the optimism and apparent talent on both sides of the ball, the Vols struggled back and forth between dominance and mediocrity in the first four games of the season.

Johnny Majors' former team, Pittsburgh, came in on opening night and spoiled the fans' fun by a score of 13 to 3.

Tennessee recovered against a weak New Mexico team the following week 31 to 6.

Then the real part of the schedule began with opponents from the Southeastern Conference. Auburn showed no politeness to their hosts when they pounded the Big Orange 37 to 14 in Knoxville.

It took a weak sister to the south, The Citadel, to give Tennessee its second win of the season, with the Vols winning by a 45 to 6 score before the west Tennessee contingent of Big Orange fans at Memphis.

There was grumbling about the coach, about the quarterback, and about the defense, as the Vols prepared for Louisiana State in Knoxville. Tennessee was a three-point underdog in their home stadium. The Vols were getting little respect.

They hadn't won against a quality opponent in their first four starts. The motto for the week was, "It's time to win a big game."

It was the third night game of the season at Neyland Stadium when the LSU Tigers came to town for the October 8 game.

Coach Majors got a near perfectly executed game from his players. The Vols had no fumbles and only one pass intercepted on a batted ball. In earlier games, Tennessee had turned the ball over too much to win.

Alan Cockrell ran the ball in from 43-yards out for one of the scores against the Tigers. With the several sacks he had had earlier in the season, which had put him in the minus category in rushing, he was delighted with the long run. "This gets me a little closer to the plus column, but I've got twenty or thirty yards to go."

Tennessee's defense also proved up to the task, limiting LSU to two field goals as the Vols finally did win a big game in the season, 20 to 6.

Knoxville *News-Sentinel* sports editor Marvin West wrote that "the thumping victory of LSU is how football is supposed to be played . . . with walloping enthusiasm. The Volunteer defense was a joy to behold, and long-suffering fans loved every minute of it. Some who usually leave early stayed to the end and sang along with the celebration concert by the Tennessee band.

"If Tennessee can play in Birmingham as it did Saturday night at Neyland Stadium, Alabama is in trouble."

That was the big **"If"** that was in everyone's mind.

The date in Birmingham would be different from the fray with the Tigers in Knoxville. The elephants had memories of the 35-28 victory by Tennessee in 1982.

Paul "Bear" Bryant retired from coaching after the 1982 season. His Crimson Tide defeated Illinois at the Liberty Bowl in Memphis for the final victory of his career—Number 323—on December 29, 1982.

It was cold and blustery at that night game near the Mississippi River which separated him from his native state of Arkansas. Fittingly, his last game was played in the state where he had tormented so many of Tennessee's football teams, not far from the state of his birth, with the state and school that he had adopted as his own.

As he leaned against the biting wind and cold, fans could see a sadness in his face, not the natural scowling look that he used so often, but a bittersweet acknowledgement that it was the end.

In less than a month, he was dead.

While Tennessee fans hated the fact that he was so successful against their Vols as Alabama's coach for twenty-five years, they always respected him. He was a rival and antagonist without peer.

Tennessee had Robert Neyland.

Alabama had Bear Bryant.

During his thirty-eight years of head coaching, which began at Maryland in 1945, then proceeded to Kentucky, Texas A&M, and finally to Alabama, his record was 323 wins, 85 losses, and 17 ties.

165

Ray Perkins took the head coaching job at Alabama after Bryant's retirement. He didn't replace the Bear. No one could.

Perkins had been an All-SEC end when he played at Alabama in 1964, 65, and 66. He was on the opposing team when Tennessee tied Alabama in 1965 at Birmingham and when the Tide won in Knoxville in 1966 because the field goal attempt sailed wide. He knew the intensity of the series.

He was chosen for the All-1960's Alabama team as a wide receiver, which in his case was a glorified end position. He is listed next to Bill Battle on that team in the Alabama media guide. Perkins had coached the New York Giants in the NFL before returning to his alma mater to take over the reins.

When he came in as coach, he was determined to be his own man and not a clone of Bear Bryant. He proved that he wasn't.

He did several things that irked Tide fans. Bear Bryant's famous tower at the practice field was removed. He engineered the replacement of John Forney who had been the Alabama play-by-play announcer for thirty years. Then he junked the wishbone offense for a faster moving pro set.

"I can't try to do things the way Coach Bryant did them," he said. "People who try to be just like someone else don't have much faith or belief in themselves. I've never known anybody to do that and be successful."

So, he would fly or crash his own way.

Alabama fans had to like the results with the opening of the season.

Georgia Tech fell 20 to 7 in Birmingham. Mississippi, almost lifeless, succumbed 40 to 0 to the Tide at Tuscaloosa. Vanderbilt scored some but lost 44 to 24 in Nashville. Memphis State offered little resistance as the Tide tamed the Tigers 44 to 13 in Tuscaloosa.

In the fifth game of the season, however, Perkins and Alabama ran into a seasoned coach and team in Joe Paterno and

Penn State at State College. Penn State prevailed 34 to 28, but only on a hotly disputed incomplete pass call that could have allowed Alabama a touchdown and possible winning opportunity.

So, Tennessee would come into Alabama week with three wins and two losses; Alabama with four wins and one hard loss. It was Perkins' first as Alabama's coach.

In the rest of the news during Alabama week, Jake Butcher was proceeding through bankruptcy liquidation but was fighting to withhold information on financial reports which might incriminate him.

Baltimore and Philadelphia were in the World Series with Baltimore leading two games to one.

Sean Connery was back in a James Bond movie "Never Say Never Again."

On October 13, NASA announced that faulty equipment on The Challenger space shuttle would delay the next launch for four months until January 1984. Two years later the craft would explode shortly after lift off.

Alabama was installed as a thirteen-point favorite by the oddsmakers at the beginning of the week. Tennessee was getting little respect despite their victory over LSU.

"Two touchdowns? They'll be doing good if they score one," said Tennessee's strong safety Joe Cofer.

Reggie McKenzie thought "our defense can stop them."

Running back Johnnie Jones was equally incredulous. "Two *points*?" he asked when he first heard the odds. "Two touchdowns? Alabama over us? Huh uh, I think our team has improved a whole lot since the first game. And I think we have a much better defense than we had when we beat them last year."

Coach Majors was voicing more confidence in his offense and defense. "Alan has put us into a lot of good plays this year, and I was certainly pleased with him in the LSU game."

And as for Reggie White, Majors called him "the most dominating lineman I've ever been around."

Redshirt freshman linebacker Dale Jones from Cleveland was beginning to get some mention. He had played exceptionally well early in the season. "It's weird," he told Knoxville *Journal* sportswriter Randy Moore. "Somehow, before the play even starts, I get a feeling that I know what hole they're going to run to. Then I try to fill it."

As for stopping Alabama, quarterback Walter Lewis was the key. He had adjusted well to the change from Bryant's wishbone to Perkins' pro set offense. He had already thrown for 1110 yards on 72 completions in 114 attempts. "He is playing some absolutely great football for us," Coach Perkins said.

The Alabama steamroller of an offense was averaging 464 yards and 35 points per game. They were ranked number eleven in the country despite their loss to Penn State.

Tennessee's Cockrell had thrown for 731 yards on 66 completions out of 124 attempts. His passes accounted for five touchdowns. Tennessee was averaging 345 yards and 23 points per game. The Vols weren't ranked in the top twenty.

Ben Byrd, Knoxville *Journal* sports editor, on the day before the game recounted some of the games and plays he had witnessed between Alabama and Tennessee. Perhaps a little bit prophetically, he recalled, "Johnny Butler's storied touchdown run in 1939 was the greatest single play I have ever seen in a Tennessee-Alabama game, or any other game for that matter . . . . Butler's run, 56 yards untouched back and forth through the entire Alabama team, provided the dash and color to what was really a one-sided game."

Game day. October 15. Tennessee had not beaten Alabama in Birmingham since 1969. Television passed on the game. Alabama was too big a favorite. It would prove to be a decision that the television networks would regret. It was to be a record-setting day.

Alan Cockrell was making his first and last trip to Legion Field. "There was pure pressure. We beat them the last year, but it was probably some kind of fluke. That's what some people were saying."

Alabama began as a top ten team should against an outmanned opponent, driving down the field. Lewis then found Joey Jones for a 31-yard touchdown pass. It would turn out to be Lewis' only touchdown pass of the day. The scoring was only beginning.

After the ensuing kickoff, Tennessee took the ball at their 20-yard line.

Cockrell describes the Vols' first play from scrimmage: "It's called an 80's passing series. I had a three-step drop. The outside receiver would run a six to eight yard route. The inside receiver would run a little seam route.

"I would read the strong safety. He can only cover one of the two receivers. He took the outside and Lenny (Taylor) was wide open. All I had to do was to get the ball there before the linebacker arrived.

"I probably threw the ball fifteen yards. Lenny turned it into an eighty-yard touchdown." It was the Vols' fourth longest touchdown pass in history. There was still over nine and a half minutes left in the first quarter.

The crowd was stunned. Tennessee had had the ball about eleven seconds, and the score was tied at seven. Cockrell and Lewis both had a touchdown pass.

The Tide behaved as though they were unaffected by the quick score. They drove, if you call an 86-yard run by Kerry Goode to the seven-yard line a drive, and fullback Ricky Moore bulldozed in from the three. Alabama 14, Tennessee 7.

Cockrell and company weren't to be outdone. This time Cockrell would do some running of his own. He still wanted to get on the plus side of the ledger for the season. After driving the Vols to the Alabama six-yard line, he took the ball on a bootleg of a type that "was one pass option. The corner came up on the

LEGACY OF THE SWAMP RAT

receiver and I just kind of walked in." Fuad Reveiz kicked his second extra point. Tennessee 14, Alabama 14.

Reggie White then sacked Lewis to end an Alabama threat.

It was the end of the first quarter, but no one left their seats for a hotdog. Back in Tennessee and outside Legion Field in other parts of Alabama, fans who had not been able to make it to the game leaned closer to the radios and called for their loved ones to come listen to a developing classic.

On the second play of the second quarter, Tennessee rushed to the line without a huddle and caught the Tide off-stride. What had been third-and-fifteen, turned into a 29-yard gain on a pass to Taylor. U-T failed to score.

After Alabama turned the ball back to the Vols, Tennessee mounted a drive but had to settle for a 28-yard Reveiz field goal. Tennessee leads 17 to 14.

The Tide never liked to be behind at half time. It meant stern talks from coaches, frowning faces, and kicked-over chairs.

Chester Braggs decided to do something about the deficit on the ensuing kickoff, returning a bad kick from his own six-yard line to the Tennessee 30. A few plays later, Lewis kept for a six-yard touchdown. Alabama 21, Tennessee 17. Lewis and Cockrell were now even—one passing and one rushing touchdown each.

Alabama got one more chance before halftime and took advantage of it with a 25-yard field goal by Van Tiffin. At the half Alabama led 24 to 17.

Just like the year before, Tennessee had Alabama right where they wanted them. This time Bama was ahead by seven instead of eight. This time Tennessee had the experience of the year before and knew they could come back. Neither team was going to shut it down.

On U-T's first play of the second half, Cockrell pitched out to where Johnnie Jones should have been. He had gone the opposite direction. Freddie Robinson recovered for Alabama. Tennessee held Bama to a field goal. There was still nine and a half minutes left in the third, but Alabama was up by ten, 27 to 17.

It was time for Cockrell and his receivers to make it interesting.

Cockrell describes Tennessee's next offensive play: "This is a hitch screen. I fake a pitch to Johnnie Jones. Clyde (Duncan) takes two steps and comes back. I throw the ball out there to him on the line of scrimmage. Curt Singer went out and knocked out the corner. Clyde out ran everyone to the end zone."

It was eighty yards of beauty for Tennessee fans. The play consumed thirteen seconds.

Those in Tennessee who had drifted away from the radio when Alabama went up by ten, returned with renewed interest as John Ward and Bill Anderson described the play again. With Reveiz's extra point, Tennessee only trailed by three, 24 to 27.

Cockrell liked that play because it allowed "guys like Curt Singer and Mike Furnas, who could run, to take on a little bitty cornerback. The receivers could always run with it."

Lennie Patrick returned the kickoff forty-six yards down the sideline. Alabama punched it in on a six-yard run by Moore on the seventh play. After the extra point, it was Alabama 34, Tennessee 24.

There was still time left in the third quarter.

Cockrell came to the line on third and long and looked over the Alabama defense. With the snap, he faked a handoff to the right. "They read it like a book. I had a fullback in the flat and my inside receiver was running a comeback route. Both those guys were covered.

"What the heck. It was third and long anyway. I thought I'd just throw the thing out there and if it got picked off, it would be as good as a punt."

Instead, Duncan out jumped Robinson for it, Robinson fell, and Duncan took it in for a 57-yard touchdown. Cockrell had three touchdowns by air, but he gave credit for all of them to his receivers and the blockers. The one to Duncan was "just kind of a luck out type of deal." Alabama 34, Tennessee 31.

The third quarter ended.

In the stadium and in thousands of homes in both states, it was time to check the purses for the nitroglycerin tablets.

The action really got thick in the fourth quarter after Reveiz kicked a 37-yard field goal to tie the game at 34.

Linebacker Dale Jones would go on to make two big fourth quarter stops. As in the past, the game came down to defense or the lack thereof.

Alabama had the ball at the Vol 14 on a third and two situation. Jones fought off a block and tripped up Joe Carter for a two yard loss. The Tide missed the field goal attempt.

Then, with the score still tied and just over four and a half minutes left in the game, Alabama has third and six near midfield.

Quarterback Lewis took the snap and handed it off to split end Greg Richardson on a sweep. It was supposed to surprise the Vols and probably would have if Jones had gone directly in on his assigned blitz. Instead, he noticed a tackle coming his way and knew something was up. He played off the block of the tackle and threw Richardson for a twelve-yard loss.

Alabama had to punt. Tennessee got the ball on their own 27 with about four minutes left. Seventy-three yards separated the Vols from a victory.

Cockrell threw a screen pass to B. B. Cooper that was good for just a yard. Johnnie Jones slammed off right tackle on a draw for six yards. That left it with three yards to go on third down. Tennessee called time out with 3:17 left in the game and the ball at their own 34. They needed enough yardage for a first down, or this would probably be the last time they would see the ball.

During the time out, the coaches discussed with Cockrell running an option. "We all thought the option would work," Cockrell said.

"That play call was a staff decision," Coach Majors would later say.

THE PLAY was "48 or opposite."

Cockrell explained it. "Well, in the huddle, I went '48 or

172

opposite at the line on three.' I went to the line. They had their defense stacked against our power side which was the short side of the field. So, instead of running 48 which would go to the right I was going to run the opposite.

"My first sound was to say 'move' to start any motion that we might have on a play. Then I went, 'OPPOSITE, OPPOSITE, OPPOSITE, hut, hut, hut' and we ran it.

"I went to my left down the line, the linebacker came down on me just like he was supposed to, and I flipped it out there to Johnnie. Lenny Taylor threw the most beautiful block I've ever seen in my life.

"Johnnie just got to run after that. That sure was a pretty sight, him scampering into the end zone."

Tim McGee, who was split out to the right, threw another block on a defensive back. Jones went around left end, cut back to the right, and went behind McGee's block untouched for a sixty-six yard touchdown. Tennessee 41, Alabama 34.

Alabama still had time, but Tennessee wasn't about to let victory be snatched from them. Reggie McKenzie sacked Lewis for a 14-yard loss, and Alvin Toles put the brakes on Kerry Goode after a short gain. Alabama punted and that was that.

The celebration was sweet. No goal posts came down; the Alabama police saw to that. Vol fans celebrated at midfield. The players celebrated in the locker room. The Vols had done the impossible in the "Football Capital of The South" as was proclaimed in big block letters on Legion Field.

"Didn't nobody pick up the pitch. I had the quarterback. Didn't nobody pick up the pitch," Alabama strong linebacker Emmanuel King explained in a very subdued Tide dressing room.

Alabama defensive coordinator Ken Donahue asked, "You want it bluntly? We played terrible defense and Alan Cockrell audibilized one great game. We were blitzing from the left side. Cockrell picked it up perfectly."

For the game, Cockrell had passed for three touchdowns and rushed for another. He had 292 yards passing on twelve completions in twenty-one attempts. With the two touchdowns against Alabama in 1982 and the four in 1983, Cockrell held the record for most scoring accounted for by a Tennessee quarterback against Alabama in victories.

Alabama got right at its average: 453 yards and 34 points. It wasn't enough.

Knoxville *Journal* sports editor Ben Byrd, who had written about the famous Johnny Butler run of 1939 on the day before this game, wrote, "Of all the big plays in this big-play game, Jones' 66-yard journey to the end zone for the decisive touchdown will be the one that lives down through the football ages at Tennessee."

He added, "I don't know if any Tennessee quarterback has ever had a better day than Alan Cockrell had in this one—three touchdowns passing, one running, two or three miles in total offense, and a masterful job of field generalship."

John Majors, in the spring of 1994, thought back on Alan Cockrell as a quarterback, "He was an outstanding quarterback. He was one of the best ones I had ever seen on high school film when we were recruiting him. He was a talented freshman. He stepped into a situation that he was forced into and performed well."

Daryl Dickey was one of the backup quarterbacks for Cockrell in 1982 and 1983. "Alan was certainly a talented player to come in and do the things he did as quickly as he did. He was a natural leader and a very gritty player.

"He loved to get down and dirty with everybody. He was a smart football player and a very good athlete."

Alan had been drafted to play baseball by Toronto when he was in high school. He forsook that opportunity then to go to Tennessee.

In the spring of 1984, he took the second chance to play pro baseball after San Francisco drafted him. He moved up from A to AA to AAA with the Giant organization over four years and several cities, including Fresno, Shreveport, and Phoenix.

174

Chris Cawood

Since 1988, he has played for the Indians and Colorado Rockies organizations. Now he is with the Sky Sox, the AAA team of the Rockies at Colorado Springs where he makes his home.

He has yet to play in the majors and doesn't really expect to now. "I like playing. I like going to the clubhouse and goofing around with the guys, knowing that I'm thirty-years-old and I still get to play a kids' game. And they pay me for it."

His wife Tameson is from Colorado Springs. Alan has two sons, Ryan who is eight and Jake who is five.

For a young man who never saw a Tennessee-Alabama game until he played in one and who knew little of the tradition, Alan Cockrell contributed mightily to that tradition and that series.

He was the last Tennessee quarterback who played against the Bear.

To sum up Alan Cockrell's accomplishments: HE NEVER LOST TO ALABAMA ON THE THIRD SATURDAY IN OCTOBER.

Career Statistics

ALAN COCKRELL

| | RUSHING | | PASSING | | |
	CARRIES	YARDS	ATTEMPTS	COMPLETIONS	TDS
1981	21	64	31	15	1
1982	53	-58	294	174	12
1983	42	-22	243	128	13
TOTALS	116	-16	568	317	26

1983

SEASON RECORDS

GAME STATS	Tennessee	Alabama
First downs rushing	12	13
First downs passing	7	13
Total first downs	19	26
Attempts rushing	50	48
Yards gained rushing	288	289
Yards lost rushing	56	81
Net yards rushing	232	208
Passes attempted	21	34
Passes completed	12	19
Passes intercepted	0	0
Net yards passing	292	245
Total yards gained	524	453

Quarterback stats	Cockrell	Lewis
Passes attempted	21	34
Passes completed	12	19
Passes intercepted	0	0
Net yards passing	292	245
Rushing attempts	9	13
Net yards rushing	-6	0
Total yards	286	245

TENNESSEE

3	Pittsburgh	13
31	New Mexico	6
14	Auburn	37
45	The Citadel	6
20	Louisiana St	6
41	Alabama	34
37	GA Tech	3
7	Rutgers	0
10	Mississippi	13
10	Kentucky	0
34	Vanderbilt	24

FLORIDA CITRUS BOWL

30	Maryland	23

ALABAMA

20	GA Tech	7
40	Mississippi	0
44	Vanderbilt	24
44	Memphis St	13
28	Penn St	34
34	Tennessee	41
35	Miss. St	18
32	LSU	26
28	Sourthern Miss.	16
13	Boston College	20
20	Auburn	23

SUN BOWL

28	SMU	7

Chris Cawood

Alan Cockrell was proficient as an eleven-year-old Punt, Pass, and Kick contestant (above) or as Tennessee's quarterback (below).

Chris Cawood

Quarterback Trivia

What are the things that the quarterbacks who won or tied against Alabama have in common? How did they differ? What about the numbers? Are there hints in the characteristics that were the same or those that differed that might point us toward the kind of quarterback who will be successful against Alabama?

In this book, the quarterbacks considered are Dewey Warren, Charlie Fulton, Bubba Wyche, Bobby Scott, Alan Cockrell, Tony Robinson, Daryl Dickey, and Heath Shuler.

First, no quarterback who was born or went to high school in Tennessee has ever led the Vols to victory over the Tide during the last thirty years. Fulton is the only Tennessean by birth or who went to high school in the state. Yet, in 1965, Alabama and Tennessee tied.

Jersey numbers? Oddly, Number 12 (Fulton) and Number 21 (Shuler) tied Alabama. They have the same numerals in their jersey numbers, only reversed. They are on either end of the series of games that we are considering (1965 and 1993).

Jersey numbers that have been worn by winning quarterbacks are 10, 6, 11, 18, and 16 for the Swamp Rat who held for extra points and the field goal in 1967.

Four starting quarterbacks accounted for two wins each in their careers and were never defeated by Alabama in a game that they started. They are Wyche, Scott, Cockrell, and Robinson. Only Scott and Robinson spent their four years at U-T with teams

179

that never tasted defeat at the hands of the Tide.

Although the game has been played on the third Saturday in October since 1928, the day of the month for the eight victories since 1967 are: the 21st, the 19th, the 18th, the 17th, the 16th, the 15th, and the 20th. There have been two wins on the 19th.

BOTH TIES WERE ON THE 16TH. Both tie scores had the numeral "7" in the scores.

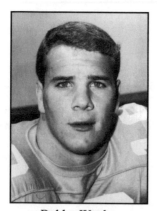

Bubba Wyche

Bobby Scott

Alan Cockrell

Tony Robinson

These four Tennessee quarterbacks won two games each over Alabama.

1984—Tony Robinson

He had an arm like a howitzer with the touch of a fly fisherman.

Kevin Altoona Robinson was the first-born child of Johnny and Jean Robinson. He was born a month after Doug Dickey made his appearance in Knoxville as the new head coach of the Volunteers. Twenty years later, Tony Robinson and Dickey's son, Daryl, would be the quarterback and the backup quarterback, respectively, for the Vols. Doug Dickey was in Florida in business.

Robinson grew up playing football on the asphalt surfaces of Tallahassee's back streets.

"In Florida, you've got to really be able to play football. Where I grew up, you got tackled in the street. We would play touch football in the middle of the street. If you ran anywhere near the sideline, you were gonna get nailed.

"There would be three or four guys coming at you. I grew up with guys that were six or seven years older than I was. They're the ones that taught me the game. That's why I love it so much. It's a rough sport. I'm a rough guy. You've got to be rough to play football."

Tony was not an only child. Johnny and Jean Robinson had five others. Tony has three brothers and two sisters.

"My mom's a preacher. My dad's a preacher also. We grew up going to church and Sunday School. We were Baptist. We

181

weren't rich or anything, but we weren't poor. We ate pretty good."

Tallahassee sits about thirty miles north of the Gulf of Mexico. It's Florida's capital city and home to the Florida State Seminoles.

Ponce de Leon is said to have explored through that part of Florida in his quest for the fountain of youth. If he found it, he forgot where it was since he died in 1521 at the age of sixty-one. There are many things in Florida named for the explorer, including the county where Tallahassee squats along I-10.

It was at Leon High School, just a long lob of Tony's arm from where he lived, that he honed his skills under Coach Gene Cox.

"My high school coach taught me a lot. I learned about setting up, having the ball where I needed it, protecting the ball when I'm dropping back, and keeping both hands on the ball. He taught me about throwing the deep ball and the short ball."

Like most of the quality athletes who make their way to big schools, Tony had excelled at baseball, basketball, and football as a youth. "My mother and father never discouraged me from playing any sport. They always wanted me to play sports."

Tony started at quarterback for the Leon Lions from his sophomore year through the end of his high school career. "We only lost three or four games the three years I played," he told an interviewer in 1993.

Florida had become a hotbed of recruiting since the state was loaded with quality players. There were enough first-class players to fill the rosters of Miami, Florida, and Florida State, not to mention other colleges of smaller enrollments. Other Southeastern Conference schools, along with those who recruited nationally, such as Notre Dame, UCLA, Southern Cal, and Penn State, dipped into the state to attempt to lure the best players to more moderate climates and playing fields.

"In Florida, you've got a bunch of good high school teams. We were big, but there were some who were bigger. My senior year in high school we were ranked Number Three in the *nation*.

We played rough ball down in Florida. It was hard for us to get games sometimes. Nobody wanted to play us."

Coach Johnny Majors heard reports from his assistant Bobby Jackson and from others who were responsible for recruiting. When he saw the film, he wasn't disappointed. In 1994, he still spoke enthusiastically of what he saw. "He had the best touch on the football that I had ever seen in a high school player."

This was quite a compliment since Majors had made a similar statement about Alan Cockrell who was a year ahead of Robinson in high school. Of course, he was correct, as those two quarterbacks would combine to help lead the Vols to four straight victories over Alabama.

Tony didn't know all that much about Tennessee, having grown up in Tallahassee. If the newspapers ever mentioned the Vols, it was usually in small box scores after the editors were sure that room wasn't needed for extra obituaries or the astrology chart.

How many schools recruited him?

"Bunches. I think every major school there is. I visited Georgia, Tennessee, Michigan, and Tulane. My first choice was Georgia. But I was prepared to go to any team that was going to pass the ball."

Coach Jackson did a fine job of recruiting and selling U-T's offense to Tony as one that he would fit in with very well.

"I visited the campus. Coach Jackson told me they were going to throw the ball, and I had a chance of starting my freshman year if I worked hard and everything."

At the time, there appeared a good chance a talented freshman could start. Alan Cockrell had blown a knee out in the Auburn game of 1981, and no one was sure in early 1982, when Robinson was being recruited, that Cockrell would rehabilitate in time to help in 1982.

The gritty Cockrell did. He had lost his jersey number to Daryl Dickey, but he wasn't going to give up the quarterback job without a fight.

Instead of starting his freshman year, Tony carried the ball three times and threw it three. He gained four yards on his carries but didn't make a single completion. That was a far cry from what he had expected to do. He got to watch Cockrell lead the team to their first victory in eleven years over Alabama.

His sophomore year was 1983. He watched again as Cockrell and the Vols made it two in a row over Bama. "I felt I was ready to take over my sophomore year, but Coach Majors didn't feel like I was ready yet. So, I just had to deal with it."

However, sometimes it was difficult to deal with. He went home. He was ready to go to work in a hardware store or anyplace where he didn't have to sit on the bench waiting his turn. "Yeah, I did leave. I got home, sat down, and talked to my parents. My father basically said, 'Look, you signed the papers to go there. You stick by your word.'"

He played out his sophomore year as a backup for Cockrell. He had nine carries for minus ten yards. He had six completions on twelve attempts. He threw his first college touchdown. In two years, he had thrown the ball a total of fifteen times. He wasn't exactly on the road to any career records. Daryl Dickey was probably aware that Robinson would jump ahead of him to the starting position in 1984 if Cockrell left for pro baseball

Cockrell's taking the baseball opportunity in the spring of 1984, gave Tony Robinson the opening he needed.

Tony never lacked confidence. "I was never nervous. I was ready to play."

A certain reporter for a Knoxville newspaper didn't share that opinion. "Before we went on the field in 1984, there was a reporter by the name of . . . who told me, 'Tony, I don't think you can run the Tennessee offense.'

"I told him, 'You don't know me.'"

The stadium awed him only momentarily. "When I first got there, I thought, 'Wow!' But once I got to playing, I focused on the field, not on the fans, because if I focused on the fans, I couldn't get my job done on the field. There was a lot of timing involved, just like an oiled machine. One step at a time. Move the clock. Move the sticks. I'd take what the defense gave me. If they gave me the home run, I went for it."

The 1984 season, though, would be anything but beautiful, especially at the start.

The Vols won the opener over Washington State at Knoxville by a touchdown, 34 to 27. When they barely edged Utah State, which is not usually thought of as a football powerhouse, by 27 to 21, the fans became restless. Army invaded Neyland Stadium and didn't stack their rifles until they tied Tennessee at 24.

Auburn and Bo Jackson were whetting their appetites in Alabama, waiting to squeeze the Big Orange. They did, 29 to 10.

Tony would have his best game of the season the following week when the Florida Gators slithered onto Shields-Watkins field. Perhaps it was because he was from Florida, but Tony came alive with an offensive show. If the Vol defense had shown up, perhaps a defeat could have been averted. It was not. Florida 43, Tennessee 30.

Ben Byrd recounted in the Knoxville *Journal* the following Monday that "Tony Robinson turned in one of the finest performances of a Vol quarterback since the switch to the T formation 20 years ago, the Vols struck early and often. One play, the 48-yard touchdown pass from Robinson to Joey Clickscales, was sure poetry — a long, high soaring pass right on the money and an over-the-shoulder catch stolen away from a Gator defender."

Alabama was suffering through its roughest start in over a quarter century. Ray Perkins, in his second year as head coach, watched as the Tide lost its first two games of the season to Boston College and Georgia Tech. The Tide beat Southwestern Louisiana 37 to 14, but then lost on consecutive weeks to lowly Vanderbilt at Tuscaloosa and Georgia in Birmingham. Three of its four losses had been televised. The week before its date with Tennnessee, Alabama did put away Penn State 6 to 0 at Tuscaloosa.

185

Walter Mondale was contesting with Ronald Reagan for the White House during Alabama week in 1984. Knoxville's Victor Ashe was running against Al Gore Jr. for the U.S. Senate.

Sally Field was starring in "Places in the Heart" at local theaters. Detroit beat San Diego in the World Series four games to one.

There was an unusual feeling during the normal festivities on the U-T campus in Knoxville in preparation for Alabama week. Tennessee had lost two games already and Alabama four. Yet, Bama was a three-point pick.

For the first time in memory, Tennessee and Alabama both were tied for last in the SEC standings. Alabama had the worst offense in the league, and Tennessee had the worst defense.

The game wouldn't be televised. There was little interest outside the two states. But still, to the players, coaches, and fans, it was Alabama versus Tennessee, which for this occasion meant it was FOOTBALL TIME IN TENNESSEE.

Byrd wrote a day before the game that despite the glitz of quarterbacks or the hype of coaches and players, the Tennessee-Alabama game "almost always comes down to the bedrock basics of blocking, tackling, and kicking." Again, he would be an accurate prophet.

For those fans who would stay to the finish, the 1984 game would prove to be one of the most exciting of the series.

Alabama powered it up the middle during its first scoring drive. They wanted to test the heart of the worst defense in the conference. Chester Braggs and Paul Carruth banged through the line for large chunks while quarterback Vince Sutton mixed in a 17-yard pass to Greg Richardson. The offense sputtered as the defense stiffened. Alabama settled for a Van Tiffin field goal. Alabama 3, Tennessee 0. There were no other threats by either team in the first quarter.

Robinson threw when he shouldn't, deep in Tennessee territory, and Louis Dean intercepted. Bama moved it eleven yards to the Vol 22-yard line before running out of steam. Tennessee aided them by jumping offsides on the Tide's field goal attempt, giving Alabama new life. Carruth caught a pass for 18-yards to the four-yard line and then ran over the left side for Alabama's first touchdown. Tiffin kicked the extra point to make it 10 to 0, Alabama.

Tennessee finally got a drive going more than a third of the way through the second quarter. Robinson teamed up with Jeff Smith for a 20-yard completion to the Bama 34. Johnnie Jones took it into the gut of Alabama's defense for thirteen yards. Jones took another pitch around the left side for seven more to the Bama 14-yard line. Robinson found Clinkscales for an eight-yard touchdown pass just a bit later. Fuad Reveiz kicked the extra point. Tennessee 7, Alabama 10.

Dale Jones had made several big plays in the Alabama game in 1983 as a freshman. This time he caused a fumble that Jim Dunkin recovered at the Alabama twelve-yard line. However, the Vols could only manage two yards in three plays. Reveiz kicked the 27-yard field goal to tie the game at ten each.

One of Alabama's favorite tactics was to respond quickly anytime it was threatened with being tied or behind at halftime with Tennessee. This year was no exception. Carruth ran left for nine yards. After another two-yard gain, Sutton threw to Richardson for sixty-six yards and a touchdown to equal Johnnie Jones run for Tennessee the year before. The Tiffin extra point gave the Tide a 17 to 10 lead at halftime.

Tennessee's old-timers could give the youngsters the "we have them right where we want them" talk of 1982 and 1983.

Instead, Coach Majors did it for them. "I told them we were playing hard. I told them we got a good break at the end of the half, but we were killing ourselves. I told them we had to play better, to be more tenacious, and to show better poise. We had a chance to win."

Alabama came out from the halftime break with other ideas. After a short punt from Tennessee All-American Jimmy Colquitt, the Tide took over at its own 45-yard line. Sutton passed to Billy Getchel who took it to the Vol 40. Don Horstead ran through the Tennessee defense for thirteen to the 27. The Tide kept on punching with Carruth running the final twelve yards for his second touchdown. The Tiffin extra point made it a two-touchdown lead at 24 to 10 in Alabama's favor.

With Alabama ahead by that much going into the fourth quarter, some Tennessee fans began to check their watches and to think about making an early exit.

Robinson and the offense would come alive in this last quarter. He passed twenty-two yards to John Cook. William Howard got a tough seven yards to the U-T 44-yard line. Robinson and Clinkscales connected on a screen pass that the receiver turned into a twenty-two-yard gain. Jones ran around right end for fifteen, but the offense failed to put it into the end zone. Reveiz kicked a 29-yard field goal to make it 13 to 24.

Just as soon as the Vols thought they were catching up, Alabama drove for seventy-one yards and killed six and a half minutes on the clock to settle for a field goal that stretched the lead to fourteen again. Alabama 27, Tennessee 13.

With eight minutes left in the game, those faint-at-heart fans started for the exits while Tony Robinson and the offense made their way onto the field. Many of those who left would have to listen to the exciting finish on their car radios.

Robinson passed for nine yards to Tim McGee to take it to the U-T 39. Another pass took it to midfield. On fourth down and needing three yards, Howard muscled it to the Alabama 47, and the official signaled a first down despite the disagreement of Tide players and coaches.

Smith caught a tight spiral from Robinson and rambled to the Alabama 19-yard line. On second-and-eight, McGee latched onto another Robinson dart for a seventeen-yard touchdown. Reveiz kicked the extra point, and Tennessee was down only by a touchdown and extra point, 20 to 27.

It would be up to the defense to give the Vols a chance to

win. Alabama would take the kickoff with just over four minutes to play. Two or three first downs could run all the time off the clock.

The defense and noise of the crowd rose to the occasion. On first down, senior co-captain Carl Zander crashed through from his linebacker position to stuff Doug Allen for no gain. On second down, Johnny McAdams and others met Horstead for the same effect. Quarterback Sutton was pressured on third down and threw incomplete toward Richardson.

Coach Majors sent in freshman Andre Creamer to receive the punt. "I was standing there clinching my fists," Creamer remembered. "I felt something big was going to happen. But I didn't know whether it would be big for them or big for me."

He cradled the spiral to his chest at the Tennessee 44-yard line. Dale Jones was back near him. "When I saw how all of them were bunched up, I knew if he got by one guy he was gone," Jones said. Tommy Sims brushed that one pursuer off Creamer.

"After that it was all green," Creamer said. He wasn't stopped for forty-five yards. He ran down the left side, near the Alabama bench, where Tide reserves and coaches could only watch his jersey Number 1 become an exclamation mark.

On first down, Jones went for six. Robinson ran for three. On third down, Jones blasted just inside the one for a first down. Then Jones followed friends and blockers Charles Wilson and B. B. Cooper on a sweep of the left side for the score. Tennessee 26, Alabama 27.

The coaching staff discussed the call. They went to the old reliable that had beaten Alabama the year before — the 48 option. It would either be Jones or Robinson who would get the opportunity to score the go-ahead points. Three yards was all that was needed.

When Alabama's outside linebacker Emmanuel King saw the same play coming toward him this time that had beaten the Tide the year before, he hesitated. "He who hesitates is lost" proved to be trite but true. The tough kid from Florida kept the ball and

189

dived into the end zone for two points and the lead.

"It was my fault, pure and simple. I was slow-playing the quarterback instead of attacking," King lamented after the game.

Tommy Sims intercepted a pass on Alabama's last series to seal the win.

For the third straight year, Tennessee had come from behind in the fourth quarter to beat Alabama. The goal posts came down again. This time it was easier. They were aluminum. There was partying on "The Strip" along Cumberland Avenue that ran through the campus. The fourth largest crowd in history, 95,422, witnessed the heart-stopping come from behind victory.

It was the first time that Alabama had been defeated three years in a row by the same team since the Tennessee run of 1967-70.

Tony Robinson was good on ten completions in twenty-three attempts for two touchdowns. His three yard nose dive for the two points would be more remembered though.

Tennessee finished out the season with four more wins and two losses, including a loss to Maryland in the Sun Bowl. Alabama, their season a disaster, lost again to have the first losing season since before Bear Bryant.

Tony Robinson would go on to set a single season total offense record of 2089 yards. Before the Alabama game in 1985, he would grace the cover of *Sports Illustrated* as Tennessee defeated Auburn. Later, his face would be pictured in profile and head on in the police files of Knoxville.

(Thanks to John Brannon of the Union City *Daily Messenger* for making interview notes with Tony Robinson from 1993 and photos available to me for use in this book. Much of this chapter and the next was based on that interview.)

Chris Cawood

1984

GAME STATS	Tennessee	Alabama
First downs rushing	10	11
First downs passing	6	7
Total first downs	16	19
Attempts rushing	44	54
Yards gained rushing	156	206
Yards lost rushing	31	15
Net yards rushing	125	191
Passes attempted	23	16
Passes completed	10	9
Passes intercepted	1	1
Net yards passing	154	178
Total yards gained	279	369

Quarterback stats	Robinson	Sutton
Passes attempted	23	15
Passes completed	10	8
Passes intercepted	1	1
Net yards passing	154	167
Rushing attempts	11	3
Net yards rushing	3	2
Total yards	157	169

TENNESSEE
34 Washington St 27
27 Utah 21
24 ARMY 24
10 Auburn 29
30 Florida 43
28 Alabama 27
24 GA Tech 21
41 Memphis St 9
41 Mississippi 17
12 Kentucky 17
29 Vanderbilt 13
   SUN BOWL
27 Maryland 28

ALABAMA
31 Boston College 38
6 GA Tech 16
37 SW Louisana 14
21 Vanderbilt 30
14 Georgia 24
6 Penn State 0
27 Tennessee 28
24 Miss. St 20
14 LSU 16
29 Cincinnati 7
17 Auburn 15

191

Tony Robinson played on the field above in Tallahassee and later helped to fill Neyland Stadium.

1985—Daryl Dickey

Except for a broken left ankle, Daryl Dickey would not have won the Most Valuable Player award in the Sugar Bowl on January 1, 1986.

Daryl made his first appearance in a Knoxville newspaper on August 24, 1964, as a two-year-old pictured with his father, Doug, mother, JoAnne, and older brothers, Don, David, and Danny. His father was preparing for his first season as head coach at Tennessee.

Daryl was born in Fayetteville, Arkansas, on June 11, 1961, while his father was an assistant at Arkansas. He attended elementary school at West Hills in Knoxville but moved to Florida when he was eight.

Being a son of a coach, he learned technique, tactics, strategy, and perseverance early. As a towel boy, or whatever, he watched his dad coach Florida from the sidelines. He was always learning.

By the time he was a sophomore at Buchholz High School in Gainesville, he became the starting quarterback. He led them to an eight and three record in the largest school classification in the state.

In 1978, his junior squad fell to four and seven with the loss of players along both lines of scrimmage from the previous year. His father left as head coach at Florida after the same season. Doug took on an assignment with Chuck Fairbanks at the

University of Colorado in Boulder.

It meant a transfer to a new school far from Florida for Daryl. He got a little jump on it though by going for the last semester of his junior year. Fairview was among the largest in classification in Colorado. There was no spring football practice for high schoolers in Colorado, so Daryl had to wait till the start of fall practice to display fully his athletic talent.

It was an odd situation. "Their quarterback was returning from the previous team that tied for the state championship."

Daryl claimed the starter's position from the first game and never let go. The other boy moved to a different position. The team won the state championship with a thirteen and one record. In that 1979 season, he made second team All-State at quarterback.

He was recruited by Tennessee and signed with the Vols in 1980.

He came to Tennessee for pre-season practice in August, 1980, while his father had left football to go into business in Florida.

Practice started a long time before classes for incoming freshmen. Shortly into practice, Daryl broke his left ankle. He could have gone to class and been redshirted for 1980.

Instead, "I, in essence, cancelled my scholarship and didn't enroll in school or start classes until January, 1981."

The rules of the NCAA, then and now, only allow a student-athlete five years from starting school work to complete four years of athletic eligibility. By waiting until January to enter school, Daryl saved himself another year in which to play ball. He would later take 1982 as a redshirt year.

His prospects to be Tennessee's starting quarterback did not brighten when the Vols signed Alan Cockrell in 1981 and Tony Robinson in 1982. Daryl did have jersey Number 11 assigned to him before Cockrell got to school, leaving Cockrell with Number 6.

Daryl's 1981 campaign amounted to one play with the varsity. He gained two yards on a keeper. His production doubled in 1983 after his redshirt year. In 1983, he carried one time for four yards and threw one incompletion.

Cockrell left after the 1983 season, electing to take his chances in baseball while feeling the footsteps of Tony Robinson thundering up from behind in the race for quarterback.

Dickey then assumed the role of backup to Robinson. In 1984, Daryl played most of the Army game while Robinson was recovering from a slight injury. The Vols were met with an Army ground game that ate up most of the clock and plays. Tennessee managed a tie at 24. For his junior year, he had a total of 41 offensive plays and seventeen pass completions. He had yet to throw a touchdown pass through three years of college.

Alan Cockrell remembers the Daryl Dickey who backed him up. "Daryl was a student of the game. He was like a coach you could go to after a series or a down. He was always into the game. On the practice field, in team meetings, or in quarterbacks' meetings, he was always trying to learn more about the game."

By the middle of September, 1985, Doug Dickey returned to Tennessee as athletic director to replace the retiring Bob Woodruff. He would get to watch his son play out his final year.

Things had changed since he left as coach after the 1969 season. "We had a 1965 preseason staff meeting, looked over the statistics, and decided we could win eight games if we averaged seventeen points and held the opposition to seventeen. I wouldn't make such a statement today. The offenses are much more potent." Dickey apparently had kept up with the scores from the Tennessee-Alabama series over the past three years.

Another significant change on the scene was the addition of Ken Donahue to the coaching staff as defensive coordinator. He was a U-T graduate but had spent twenty-one years at Alabama. He and Jim Goostree had always been the impetus behind getting Alabama ready to play Tennessee and the celebrations in the locker room after Alabama victories.

Both Tennessee and Alabama were recovering nicely from their below par seasons of 1984. Coach Ray Perkins was on the hot seat for having the first losing season at Alabama since J. B. "Ears" Whitworth had three losing seasons in a row from 1955 through 1957. He didn't want to be known as "Ears" Perkins.

Coach Johnny Majors' situation wasn't hardly as bad since his Volunteers had defeated the Tide three years in a row and were gunning for the fourth.

Perkins' Alabama squad put together four wins in a row to move into the top ten. They defeated Georgia 20 to 16, Texas A&M 23 to 10, Cincinnati 45 to 10, and Vanderbilt 40 to 20, before losing to Penn State 17 to 19.

Majors' Volunteers tied UCLA on opening night with 26 each, but bounced back to defeat Auburn 38 to 20 and Wake Forest 31 to 29, before losing to Florida 10 to 17 the week prior to their date with the Crimson Tide.

Most appropriately, Michael J. Fox was starring in "Back to the Future" at local theaters during Alabama week in Knoxville. That was just what the Vols were seeking—four in a row over Alabama as in the series from 1967 through 1970.

In other news, Andrew Thornton, who buddied with Kentucky blue-bloods, parachuted in the dark of night into south Knoxville with seventy-five pounds of cocaine strapped to his waist. He was found dead in a driveway after leaving a trail of drops over north Georgia.

The other kind of coke, Coca Cola, had seen its "New Coke" nose dive in sales compared to "Classic Coke."

"Golden Girls" was proving to be a successful new program for NBC. Kansas City with George Brett was playing St. Louis with Jack Clark in the World Series.

Former President Gerald Ford stopped by to visit with Coach Majors on Wednesday of Alabama week.

196

Both Tennessee and Alabama had an abundance of talented players ready to do battle in this annual clash.

Tony Robinson was ranked fifth nationally in passing efficiency. He had moved into sixth place in total career offense for Tennessee, just behind Dewey Warren and Bobby Scott.The Tide's Mike Shula, son of Miami Dolphin Coach Don Shula, was ranked first in passing efficiency. Alabama had Cornelius Bennett at linebacker. Tennessee had Dale Jones. Defensive back Chris White of Tennessee had four interceptions over the first four games to place him at second in the nation. Tim McGee and Joey Clinkscales were two of Robinson's favorite receivers.

Was the Tennessee-Alabama series still special to Alabama coaches and players? Trainer Goostree answered in an interview with *News-Sentinel* columnist Al Browning: "Football in our part of the nation, being the premier sport, culminates each year with a game like the one we are about to witness. The participants, players, fans, and students, whether or not they are natives of Tennessee or Alabama, get caught up in the tradition and the magnitude of what being a part of this special weekend has been in the past, is at the present, and will be in the future.

"Personally, I love this series. I get fired up. To consider it anything other than special has never entered my mind."

Tennessee was ranked twentieth and Albama fifteenth by AP. Bama was a three-point favorite.

Daryl Dickey was at his customary place on the sideline when the game started. There was no reason to believe he would be any other place during the most heated game of the year.

Unlike the previous three years, this game would be more in the traditional mode of a defensive struggle rather than a bomb fest of points. Both teams would move the ball considerably, but mainly between the twenty yard lines. Doug Dickey's analysis of what was necessary in 1965 would become reality once again.

The teams tested each other in the opening quarter but no one scored.

In the second, Tennessee got on the board first with an eighty-yard drive that took over eight minutes off the clock. Keith Davis, the Nashville freshman, ran for thirteen. Robinson had a nice pass to Charles Wilson for nine.

On third down at the Vol 47, Robinson passed again to Davis for a pass and run of twenty-five yards to the Alabama 28-yard line. Wilson bulldozed for eight, and Davis sliced through for another ten. A pass interference call gave Tennessee the ball at the two-yard line. Wilson punched it across, and Carlos Reveiz kicked the extra point. Tennessee 7, Alabama 0.

Now that the combatants had felt each other out, Alabama responded with an eighty-yard drive of its own. Murry Hill picked up large chunks of yardage. On third and ten at the Volunteer 45, Mike Shula hit Greg Richardson for 44 yards to the one-yard line. Craig Turner got the touchdown, and Van Tiffin kicked the extra point.

Tennessee's Charles Davis responded by intercepting a Shula pass at the Vol 39. Keith Davis ran for twelve. Robinson passed another twelve to Wilson. Davis again battered the line on two runs, gaining eight. With fourth-and-two at the Bama 21-yard line, Reveiz kicked a 38-yard field goal. Tennessee 10, Alabama 7, at halftime.

The Volunteer players had never led the Tide at halftime during the three previous years. They always had to come from behind. The coaches had to adjust any pep talks to remind the Vols not to become over confident. Alabama would storm back, they were sure.

In the third quarter, Tennessee was backed up deep at its own ten-yard line after an Alabama punt. However, Robinson kept for seven on third down to give the Vols a first down. He then passed to Davis for ten and kept for another eleven to move the Vols out to their own 46. Robinson threw to Wilson for nine, and a personal foul moved the ball to the Bama 30. There Tennessee stalled but was able to get a 48-yard Reveiz field goal. Tennessee 13, Alabama 7.

Robinson suffered a minor injury and had to be taken from the game for a play. Dickey came in. He got his chance to pass. Mistake. The ball went right into the hands of defensive back Ricky Thomas of Alabama. Fortunately, Thomas was not expecting the ball and dropped it.

"That guy should have intercepted the ball, " Dickey said later. "Totally my fault. That was an audible. I made the correct call, but I threw the ball to the wrong side."

Robinson came back in on the next series. Dale Jones recovered a Bobby Humphrey fumble at the Tide 28. Robinson passed ten yards to Wilson, and then ran fourteen on an option to the Alabama eight-yard line. Then it happened.

This is the way Robinson described it recently: "It was a pass play out of a power set, designed to go to running back Charles Wilson or to secondary receiver Tim McGee. When I made the fake and looked at Charles, he was covered outside in the flat. I looked inside for McGee, but he was covered.

"I saw a hole in the middle, and I thought I could run the ball, maybe even score. I was hit right on the knee. I remember Cornelius Bennett was chasing me, and he ended up on my back. A guy jumped right into my knee.

"Cornelius told me, 'T. Rob, stay down. You're hurt.' I told him I wasn't hurt, but he said, 'Yes, you are. Stay down.'

"A couple of our trainers helped me off the field. I wasn't in pain. The doctor checked my knee, looked at the trainer, and shook his head."

Tony Robinson would not play another down of football for Tennessee. His career stats still have him behind Bobby Scott. He edged ahead of Dewey Warren by eight yards. Except for the injury, he would have jumped to first place on the list by the end of the year if he had continued to average what he had to that point.

At the beginning of the fourth quarter, which Tide players always said belonged to them, the brunt of carrying Tennessee to victory fell into the hands of Daryl Dickey and the Vol defense.

It was third down. Daryl handed the ball off on a draw. Reveiz kicked a twenty-eight-yard field goal.

It was on the next series that Daryl really got his taste of what the Alabama-Tennessee rivalry was like to play in. "I really got a wake-up call. When I went in, I handed the ball off. Then in a play or two, it was time for us to throw. That's when the realization of the football game hit me.

"The thing that I will always remember very vividly was the speed of the game. It was absolutely tremendous. I dropped back to pass on a five-step drop, and literally, the defense was already beyond me by the time I got back there. It was all I could do just to throw the ball. I didn't know where I was throwing it. I just threw it.

"After I shook that off in a play or two, I began to get the feel of the speed of the game and ended up playing decently after that. I'll never forget that experience."

He wasn't asked to do much. Coach Majors and offensive coordinator Walt Harris simplified the offense to let Dickey concentrate on basic plays. They were ahead by nine and didn't need any more points if the defense could contain the Tide.

Alabama drove. Humphrey returned the kickoff to the 39. Shula hit Thornton Chandler for twelve yards and then Turner for six. Humphrey ran for a few more, and Shula threw to Chandler again for twenty to the Vol 19-yard line. Humphrey caught Shula's pass for a TD on first down. Tiffin added the extra point. Bama was just a field goal from victory at 16 to 14.

With 7:43 to go in the game, the Tide was once again driving into Tennessee territory, needing only the field goal for a win. Shula took the snap on the Vol 37-yard line. He straightened up and threw a short pass to his left in the general direction of fullback Craig Turner.

Dale Jones was in between, just yards from Shula. Jones batted the ball up and then grabbed it, the sweetest piece of leather he had ever caressed. Vol fans who saw it, or who have seen it, will remember it as one of the greatest defensive plays in the great rivalry. It was Jones' only interception of his career. It was enough. It was a career in itself.

Coach John Majors in 1994 still described it as "one of the greatest defensive plays ever in college."

Jones agreed. "That's probably my favorite play ever," he said in a bit of understatement.

Alabama would get another opportunity. With just a tick over four minutes left in the game, the Tide had fourth-and-four at the Tennessee 47-yard line. Perkins could have ordered a punt to back up Tennessee deep in its own territory and put pressure on newcomer Dickey. Instead, they went for a pass and missed.

Dickey came in and drove the Vols down field for the next three-and-a-half minutes.

Bama got the ball back with just twenty-four seconds remaining. A twenty-three yard pass put the ball on the Vol 44. Tiffin attempted a 61-yard field goal that fell about nine feet short.

Tennessee had won four in a row. They were all different. They were all exciting. Majors won't pick a favorite. "They were all exciting and meant something different at the time."

Daryl Dickey had done what was necessary. His statistics weren't monumental. But the results were. He completed one of five passes and gained five yards on one rushing attempt.

There to greet him in the dressing room was his dad, Tennessee Athletic Director Doug Dickey. It had to be special for a father to see a son who had been two-years-old when he became head coach help beat an Alabama team twenty-one years later.

Robinson's knee was operated on the next week.

The quarterback job was Dickey's if he could handle it. "I have confidence in my ability. I've worked hard, and I have to keep working hard to carry us all the way to the Sugar Bowl," he told a reporter.

The following week was a little shaky as the Vols tied Georgia Tech with six each.

201

Then, as Dickey became adjusted to the job, the Vols rolled over Rutgers, Memphis State, Mississippi, Kentucky, and Vanderbilt for five victories in November.

"Daryl had tremendous growth from the Alabama game on. He just got better and better," Coach Majors said in 1994.

Phil Fulmer remembered Daryl as a player who "paid his dues and knew a lot about what was going on. He had a lot of confidence in himself. Him winning the MVP in the Sugar Bowl is just one of the great stories in Tennessee football history."

Florida was ineligible for the championship. Tennessee won its first SEC title since 1969. They would get an opportunity to play Miami in the Sugar Bowl, which would be another game among the top ten favorites of the past quarter century in most Vol fans' minds.

The Vols rolled over the highly rated and Number One talking mouths of the Hurricanes on New Year's night in New Orleans.

Daryl Dickey, who hung around for five and a half years waiting on his opportunity, was named Most Valuable Player in the 35 to 7 slaying of the 'Canes. "It was a dream come true, because if you've done that, your team has been successful."

Yet, if he had not had the broken ankle in preseason practice in 1980, Daryl Dickey would have used up his eligibility in 1984 and not have been around for the 1985 season. People called him a "fifth-year senior," but in reality, it had been six years before when he was signed by Tennessee. He gave up his scholarship to save a year's eligibility.

Daryl now lives in Lexington, Kentucky, where he is the offensive coordinator for Bill Curry's Kentucky Wildcats. He was drafted by the San Diego Chargers out of college, injured a knee, and never played professional ball.

He came back to Tennessee as a graduate assistant in 1987. In 1988, he hooked up with the Milano Rhinos in Italy as a coach.

Chris White and Mike Furnas were playing there. He came back that fall as a volunteer coach at Tennessee and helped Walt Harris with the quarterbacks. From there he went to Florida State and then to Kentucky in the winter of 1990.

He married a girl from the Halls Community outside of Knoxville. He and Kendall have two children. Daughter Karis is four, and son Dallas James will be two in November.

"The Tennessee-Alabama series is one of the greatest rivalries that there is in football. I'm honored to have played in it."

On a cold, gusty day after spring practice at Kentucky in 1994, he was asked to describe the qualities he would look for in a quarterback. "Quarterbacks have to be natural leaders. They have to know how to take charge and play intelligent football. They have to be good athletes and good throwers. You're talking about a complete football player."

No one could have described Daryl Dickey any better.

"Someday, I hope to be able to return and help coach at the University of Tennessee," he ended.

Tony Robinson "was a tremendous talent and great football player. He had one of the best throwing arms I've ever been around or seen. He had football smarts," Daryl Dickey observed.

"Tennessee fans should be happy that Tony Robinson was around for a season and a half. We probably won't ever see his likes around here again," Russ Bebb of the Knoxville *Journal* wrote on the Monday following Tennessee's 1985 victory.

Coach John Majors, reflecting on Robinson's talents from his Pitt office in the spring of 1994, remembered a "spectacular, fabulous athlete. He had the best touch on the football of any high school player I had ever seen. In college, he was the best since Joe Namath."

The Swamp Rat also saw Robinson play. "Tony was a big, tall, rangy kid. Had a great arm. I thought he had one of the best arms that I had ever seen until Number 21 came along. Tony was exciting. He could make things happen."

Tony Robinson now lives on a deadend street, one house from the end—literally and figuratively. At thirty, he is loading and unloading furniture in Tallahassee. It's honest work but nothing like what he could have done with his talent.

After his knee injury in the 1985 Alabama game, things continued to go downhill for the quarterback who Coach Majors thought "was the best since Joe Namath." Tony went to the Sugar Bowl with the team and celebrated the Vols' victory over Miami. He was interviewed on the sidelines by television announcers. He would be back he assured them from his crutches.

Later in January he was arrested, along with B. B. Cooper, on drug charges related to possession and sale of cocaine. He pled guilty in November and was sentenced to six years. He only had to serve ninety days on the Knox County penal farm and then he would be released on probation.

Several people who knew Tony during those times relate that he "had trouble following the rules. He was given several chances."

By February, 1987, he had violated the rules of probation and was brought in to serve six months. After he was released again, he was charged with forgery. His probation was revoked, and he was sent to Brushy Mountain and then to west Tennessee. He was released in 1993 and now lives with his parents about two miles from Leon High School where his exploits had attracted many college coaches.

In an interview just before he was released from prison, Tony had this advice for young people: "Watch your friends. Don't ever be a follower. Always be a leader. Most of all, listen to your authorities. Listen to your parents and teachers."

As for his time at Tennessee, "They'll know I've been there. I don't have anything against Tennessee at all. People in Tennessee have treated me good. I appreciate that. I just wish things would have turned out differently."

1985

	LINEUPS			SEASON RECORDS

LINEUPS

SEASON RECORDS

		TENNESSEE	ALABAMA
Offensive	TE	Smith	Chandler
	T	Douglas	Johnson
	T	Wilkerson	Rose
	G	Galbreath	Condon
	G	Williams	Gilmer
	C	Kirk	Neighbors
	QB	Robinson	Shula
	FB	Henderson	Turner
	TB	Davis	Braggs
	WR	McGee	Bell
	WR	Swanson	Whitehurst
Defensive	LB	Kimbro	Rockwell
	T	Scott	Hand
	T	Hovanis	Sowell
	MG	Brown	Jarvis
	LB	Jones	Godwin
	LB	Ziegler	Davis
	LB	Miller	Thomas
	CB	Brown	Wilkinson
	CB	Creamer	Robinson
	SS	White	Thomas
	FS	Davis	Turner

TENNESSEE

26	UCLA	26
38	Auburn	20
31	Wake Forrest	29
10	Florida	17
16	Alabama	14
6	GA Tech	6
40	Rutgers	0
17	Memphis St	7
34	Mississippi	14
42	Kentucky	0
30	Vanderbilt	0

SUGAR BOWL

35	Miami	7

ALABAMA

20	Georgia	16
23	Texas A&M	10
45	Cincinnati	10
40	Vanderbilt	20
17	Penn State	19
14	Tennessee	16
28	Memphis St	9
44	Miss. State	28
14	LSU	14
24	Southern Miss	13
25	Auburn	23

ALOHA BOWL

24	Southern Cal	3

GAME STATS	Tennessee	Alabama
First downs rushing	12	10
First downs passing	8	10
Total first downs	21	22
Attempts rushing	52	33
Net yards rushing	218	139
Passes attempted	24	29
passes completed	11	16
Passes intercepted	1	2
Net yards passing	132	216
Total yards gained	350	355

Quarterback stats	Robinson	Dickey	Shula
Passes attempted	19	5	29
Passes completed	10	1	16
Passes intercepted	1	0	2
Net yards passing	130	2	216
Rushing attempts	7	1	1
Net yards rushing	22	5	2
Total yards	152	7	218

Career Statistics

Tony Robinson

	RUSHING			PASSING		
---	CARRIES	YARDS	ATTEMPTS	COMPLETIONS	TD'S
1982	3	4	3	0	0
1983	9	-10	12	6	1
1984	78	126	253	156	14
1985	44	75	143	91	8
TOTALS	134	195	411	253	23

Daryl Dickey

	RUSHING			PASSING		
---	CARRIES	YARDS	ATTEMPTS	COMPLETIONS	TD'S
1981	1	2	0		
1983	1	4	1	0	0
1984	11	10	30	17	0
1985	29	4	131	85	10
TOTALS	42	20	162	102	10

From Fairview High School, **Daryl Dickey** came to U-T and eventually won the MVP award in the 1986 Sugar Bowl. He is now offensive coordinator at Kentucky.

From Leon High School, **Tony Robinson** went to stardom at U-T and the cover of *Sports Illustrated*. He was last photographed with a football in the uniform of the Tennessee Department of Corrections in 1993.

Phillip Fulmer

Franklin County borders Alabama in mid-south Tennessee. Phillip Fulmer knew a lot about the legacy of Bear Bryant while he was going to school and playing football at Franklin County High.

Alabama, along with Georgia and Vanderbilt, was among the schools he visited on recruiting trips in 1967. There were rumors that Bear Bryant was nearing retirement. He had lost to Tennessee in 1967 and people had begun to write his obituary. Fulmer said no to Bryant of Alabama, Vince Dooley of Georgia, and Vanderbilt. A good Tennessee boy could do no better than the in-state school. "The bottom line was that I was a Tennessean and I wanted to be at the University of Tennessee."

Fulmer was a tight end and linebacker out of high school, but a nagging ankle injury slowed him in his freshman year at Tennessee. Besides, there were other linebackers there and some coming in who would have been difficult to compete with if he had had two good wheels. Steve Kiner, Jack Reynolds, Jackie Walker, Ray Nettles, and Jamie Rotella were crowding the roster.

"I was just looking for a place that I could contribute the quickest," he said.

He got to observe the Tennessee-Alabama rivalry as a player from the viewpoint of both winning and losing. He was a freshman and ineligible when Bubba Wyche and the Vols made it two in a row in 1968. His long time friend Bobby Scott and some great defensive players led Tennessee to two more victories in 1969 and 1970. Fulmer finished up his playing days against Alabama in 1971 in the first of eleven straight losses to the Tide.

The Alabama series was to him, then and now, "the greatest rivalry. We didn't get so hyped up about it that we lost our focus on it. Bama Week was always a very big time for us."

He remembers playing across the line from Alabama's All-Conference defensive tackle Terry Rowell in 1969. "It was a fun game. It was a good day."

He played at about 214 pounds. Now he can laugh about his size compared to what offensive guards weigh on the teams he has coached. Technique was more important than size. He learned his lessons well.

He saw a change in coaching from Doug Dickey to Bill Battle from the perspective of a player. That experience would suit him well when he took over from Johnny Majors as Tennessee's new head coach in late 1992.

He was prepared. He coached at Wichita State and Vanderbilt before returning to Tennessee for good in 1980. He built offensive lines from young men, many of whom would later make a living in the NFL. He moved up the ladder to assistant head coach and then to offensive coordinator before assuming the reins of a pressure packed job.

What's different about being a head coach rather than being an assistant?

"Well, as an assistant, you work very hard. As a head coach, you work very hard. So there's not much difference in that. The focus has to be on the overall team for the head coach rather than just on your position. You have to be very careful that you not let outside sources drag you away from the people that are most important—that's your family, your team, and your coaches."

Would it be more difficult for a freshman quarterback to start now than when Alan Cockrell did in 1981?

"Yes. I think the offensive scheme is more complicated, and I think defensive structures are more complicated. So, it would be harder. You could do it."

Coach Fulmer will be leading the team as head coach for the second year when Alabama comes to Neyland Stadium on October 15, 1994. Heath Shuler is gone. The quarterbacking duties will fall to Jerry Colquitt, Todd Helton, or perhaps one of the highly touted freshmen.

Chris Cawood

Head Coach **_Phillip Fulmer_** is constantly busy whether
on the field or in his office near Neyland Stadium.

211

This sign is near Swain County High School in Bryson City, North Carolina. Below, Coach Boyce Deitz stands next to **Heath Shuler's** retired jersey and sign commemorating three straight state championships.

Chris Cawood

1993—Heath Shuler

The "road to nowhere" took Heath Shuler every place he wanted to go.

Local folks put up the sign just a few miles from Heath's home near the road as it enters the Smoky Mountain National Park. Just seven miles from his home, the road ends near a tunnel. The sign says "Road Closed." It should read: "Road Ends—Never To Be Built."

It's a nice tunnel. Hikers can still walk through. It's wide enough for two lanes of traffic, cool, with the sound of dripping water keeping a steady beat. By the time a hiker reaches the center of the quarter-mile tube of concrete, the darkness envelops and the question arises: "Proceed forward or go back?"

Heath liked the tunnel. "I would go in it a lot of times at night just to scare people," he said and smiled, still a bit of mischievous boy inside a professional athlete's body.

The mountains also proved inviting. The beauty. The serenity. It was near here, at a peaceful overlook of Fontana Lake, that Heath came to think and to make some of the decisions that were important in his life. Since high school, he has had to make several.

This area of western North Carolina, where Bryson City hunches up against the mountains, was at one time more isolated than it is now. The crass commercialization hasn't caught up with the neat little town in the same way it has with Pigeon Forge and Gatlinburg on the other side of the mountains, although it appears it is headed that way.

More than a century ago, many families of German heritage

213

settled in the coves and valleys abutting the towering mountains. Among these were the Deitz's, the Maennle's, and the Shuler's. Many of the families had migrated up from Charleston, South Carolina, to find places where land was abundant and cheap. Their search ended in what is now Swain County, North Carolina.

A large share of the county's land is now off the tax rolls. There's the Smoky Mountains, the Cherokee Reservation, the land taken for Fontana Lake, plus the U.S. Forest Service has a large hunk of the mountains.

When the country needed more power to produce aluminum for World War II, Fontana Dam was built in record time. The government promised Swain Countians a road across the mountains on the south boundary of the Smokies. Instead they got seven miles of road and a tunnel that goes nowhere. Swain Countians haven't forgotten.

When Heath was born to Marge and Joe Benny Shuler, horns sounded, fireworks blasted skyward, people hugged and kissed, and there was dancing in the streets of New York and in Jackson Square in New Orleans. It helped that it was New Year's Eve in 1971.

Heath's father was a good athlete in high school but injuries kept him from college competition. Heath grew up in a family that stressed values and doing the best with the talent that God gives. "Keep your trust and faith in God, and all things will work out and you will accomplish a lot," was his mother's basic advice to Heath as he was growing up.

Western North Carolina had good football before Shuler. The University of Tennessee had plucked another talented quarterback from the area in the mid-1970's with Jimmy Streater. Shuler's High School Coach, Boyce Deitz, was an assistant at Sylva, North Carolina, when Streater led that school to the state championship.

Deitz knew he had a winner in Heath early on. The trouble was, he couldn't convince the recruiters at the University of Tennessee. "I told them we had a great quarterback over here. He was a great player. The assistant talked like and acted like it was just another high school coach calling him."

That call was made after Heath's sophomore year at Swain County High. He had just led the school to a state championship in 1-A classification. Deitz thought that was the problem. Swain County High had about 340 students, and half of those were girls. How good can a quarterback be from a backwoods school which has barely a hundred and fifty boys?

"It's ignorance. That's what it is," Deitz said emphatically. "This is a good football area. Five of the six top teams last year in Western North Carolina were in our classification."

If Tennessee wasn't interested, there were schools that were. North Carolina and North Carolina State played the suiter early. Alabama had a strong advocate in a teacher that Heath respected. In all, sixty-four schools would offer him a scholarship when he finished his high school career.

Heath took it all in stride. He talked with those he thought knowledgeable, his coaches, his family, and friends. In the meantime, he would have fun, play ball, and do some hunting.

By the time his senior season started in 1990, Tennessee was in the hunt for his services. The game at Robinsville would be the first time that college coaches could scout a game in person. It turned into a fiasco.

It was raining when Coach Deitz told his players to be sure and bring both their practice jerseys and pants and their game uniform. He wanted them to look good. And he wanted them to appear clean. They would warm up in the practice clothes and change into their sparkling maroon and white game uniforms immediately before kickoff.

Heath forgot his game pants. When he went in after warmups to change, he made the discovery. He more or less made a reserve player give him his. "You got to give me your pants. Yeah, really. You got to give me your pants. And don't tell Coach Deitz."

The reserve was sitting there with no pants when Coach

Deitz came in for the pre-game talk. "I went over and got on that boy like you've never heard. I absolutely blasted him."

With Heath properly suited out in the other boy's pants, the Maroon Devils took the field to find that Robinsville had deployed ten defensive backs. They did not intend to let Heath Shuler put on a passing show for the coaches that were there scouting. Alabama had someone, North Carolina had its head coach, and Tennessee had sent assistant David Cutcliffe.

Instead of seeing Heath pass, they saw him run. "I ran for about a hundred and fifty yards that night. Coach Deitz told me to stand there and act like I was going to throw and whenever the defense was twenty yards off me, I should start to run."

Despite the lack of a passing spectacular at Robinsville, the schools' representatives knew Shuler was a keeper.

By mid-season, Heath was culling out the schools he wasn't interested in visiting or attending. He didn't want to hurt anyone's feelings. So, he told the schools that didn't make the final cut simply, "We have narrowed it down, and you just weren't a part of the final five."

Those in the lucky final five were Alabama, North Carolina, Florida, Notre Dame, and Tennessee.

He was invited to Knoxville for the Tennessee-Notre Dame game. Notre Dame won 34 to 29 in a very exciting game. However, when he visited Notre Dame, he marked them off his list. "It wasn't what I expected. The facilities at Swain County High School were greater than the facilities at Notre Dame."

Alabama, North Carolina, and Tennessee made the final three.

His visit to Alabama was impressive. It was more relaxed than some other schools. He got a more in depth look at a fewer things instead of a rushed up peek at everything. That suited his style.

Alabama had a special little treat for him that was perfectly legal at the time, according to an NCAA representative. Heath wasn't too sure. Alabama showed him a video production of

216

Kenny Stabler and Joe Namath talking directly into the camera to him. They told him about what he could accomplish at Alabama and, at least subliminally, reminded him that they hadn't done too badly in college and professional ranks.

"I think he would have signed with Alabama if he could have done it then," Coach Deitz said in 1994. "But it wasn't signing time, and by the time it was, Tennessee was more of a factor."

Heath continued to be a model student and athlete. The only incident of somewhat inappropriate behavior that Coach Deitz could remember was the pie fight. A local store owner would, on occasion, bring to the field house dressing room pies and cakes for the players to have after practice.

"There were about twenty pies there one day," Heath remembers. "We were just goofing off, and I took a cream pie and put it in my friend's face. He chased me down and got some cherry pie on me. I got another pie when I thought my friend was coming back through the door and caught him right in the face with it. It wasn't my friend. It was Coach (Frank) Maennle. I got him good.

"Coach Deitz came in when I was in the process of throwing another one. We were supposed to eat at church that night, and he wouldn't let me go eat at the church. I had to stay there and clean up."

Coach Deitz remembers the incident also. "I'm so particular on cleanliness. It really made me mad. The ring leader was Heath."

His high school record is a standard for some other aspiring North Carolina school boy to shoot for. He led Swain to three straight state championships. He threw 42 touchdown passes his senior year and 74 for his career. He was rated the Number One high school prospect by several publications.

He also excelled in other athletic endeavors. He won the state high jump title with an effort of six feet nine inches. He played catcher and hit for a .390 average for the baseball team.

When it came time to make a decision among the three finalists, Heath weighed the pros and cons of each school with his parents, coaches, and friends. The decision would be his.

His calculus and statistics teacher wanted him to go to Alabama. "He and I were very, very close. We'd talk about recruiting and Alabama. He and Gene Stallings became close friends."

Except for the Tennessee-Notre Dame game, Heath had only seen one other Tennessee game. "My sophomore year in high school, I watched Tennessee play Kentucky in the rain."

The facilities, proximity, Coach David Cutcliffe, and one other thing tipped the balance to Tennessee. It was the opportunity NOT to play his freshman year. "I wanted a year to mature myself and be behind a good quarterback. I wanted to come to Tennessee and play behind Andy (Kelly) a year. I could have gone to Alabama and started right off. I think it's a bigger transition from high school to college than from college to pros."

He signed with Tennessee. He liked everything about it except the Alabama thing—the rivalry. "It was something negative. I got here, and it seemed like everything was riding on whether or not we beat Alabama. I hated that. That absolutely discouraged me. In one drill we had to say 'out-Bama' everytime we hit. I didn't like that. I wanted everybody else to be saying Tennessee when they hit the ground. I wanted us to be above everyone else."

Heath's intensity was such that he didn't need any special rivalry or motivation to play at the top level. He would give all whether he was playing Alabama or Vanderbilt. "I was up the same every game, regardless of whom we played."

He understood, though, the fans' perspective on the series. "A fan is different than a player. If I were a fan, I'd be saying the same thing."

Heath only lacked one thing when he came to Tennessee as

a quarterback. He had the physical attributes—about six feet two inches and 210 pounds. He had the nerve and intelligence. He would take control in the huddle and take no second-guessing from a lineman. But he sometimes threw too hard.

There are stories about him bending face masks with throws that weren't caught and breaking a plexi-glass screen in front of a television camera. Receivers became tattooed with little crosses where the point of the ball had met their skin at a velocity beyond their ability to catch.

"I got here to U-T, and I was thinking, wow, my wide receivers in high school caught better than the ones here. Of course, I had been working every day with those guys. I thought I should bring them all over to show these guys how to catch. But it just took a little time. I had to learn to be patient and lay the ball out there for them to make the great catch. Tennessee's receivers did have great hands. It just took us a while to adjust."

He got his wish to watch Andy Kelly in 1991. He passed a total of four times with two completions and one touchdown. The two completions and touchdown came in the Vanderbilt game. He carried the ball seven times for twenty-four yards. It was the season of the great win against Notre Dame at South Bend and the great losses to Alabama, 19 to 24, and Penn State in the Fiesta Bowl.

The 1992 season was an ending and a beginning. Coach Johnny Majors' health problems sidelined him for the first three games. Assistant Head Coach Phillip Fulmer, who had been at Tennessee both as a player and assistant coach, took over the reins and directed the team to three straight victories over Southwestern Louisiana, Georgia, and Florida. Majors returned in time for victories over Cincinnati and LSU.

Then came the undoing of the Majors era and the beginning of a new one. Arkansas came to Knoxville and won by a point the week before Alabama was to be there. Some fans said the coaches and players mistook the red and white of Arkansas and the "A" in their name for Alabama.

Majors would get a chance to save his job against Alabama. It would be difficult to push him out the door if the Vols won. It wasn't to be though. Alabama came into the game undefeated and ranked at Number Four in the nation. Tennessee had only lost to Arkansas and was ranked seventeenth.

What does Heath Shuler remember about the 1992 Alabama game? A concussion. "When Lemanski Hall hit me from behind, it was legitimate." It was the last quarter. Heath ran almost on autopilot after that.

"I audibled one time. I mean if I had checked off to a play a hundred times, it wouldn't have been to that one. It was a non-successful play. The hardest thing was finding my car after the game. I had no idea where I had parked it."

Alabama won, 17 to 10. To rub salt into the wound, South Carolina made it three losses in a row for the Vols two weeks later. The handwriting was on the wall, and it was etched in bold italic on orange relief.

By the time Johnny Majors reached Memphis for the game with Memphis State on November 14, the papers were on the table and ready to sign. He would leave after the season.

In the final analysis, Coach Majors decided not to coach the Hall of Fame Bowl game in Tampa. Phillip Fulmer, who had been named the next head coach, took over early.

Shuler passed superbly in the bowl, was given national exposure, and was positioned for a race at the Heisman in 1993. Over the season he had thrown for ten touchdowns and rushed for eleven more. He had accounted for 1998 total yards of offense.

Alabama loomed ahead in the thoughts of fans, if not in Heath's, as Coach Fulmer took over for his first full year.

Shuler had to look forward to this year and the teams the Vols would play. He would get a second chance at the three teams they didn't beat in 1992—Arkansas, Alabama, and South Carolina. He never let one bad play or game bother him.

220

"When he made a bad play, it was over. He didn't worry about that play. When he made the decision to go to Tennessee, the second he made it, that was the best decision he ever made. He never second-guessed himself," Coach Deitz recalled.

With Shuler's ability and the supporting cast, Vol fans maintained high hopes for the season. Aaron Hayden, James Stewart, and Charlie Garner would provide an elusive, powerful, and speedy running attack to balance Heath's passing. Craig Faulkner and Cory Fleming were senior receivers who were trusty and had soft hands.

The new kid on the block of receivers, Billy Williams, promised to add a bit of flair and daring with high leaps and acrobatic catches. Shuler would set up passing shop behind a huge and talented offensive line that included Bubba Miller, Jason Layman, Kevin Mays, and Jeff Smith.

On defense, the line looked solid, and the linebackers mean. The defensive backs would be tested early. Shane Burton, James Wilson, Horace Morris, and Paul Yatkowski anchored the defensive line. Reggie Ingram and Ben Talley patrolled at linebacker. Jason Parker, Shawn Summers, Ronald Davis, and DeRon Jenkins roamed the secondary.

The kicking game was on a solid foot with John Becksvoort and holder Lance Wheaton.

Tennessee began the season scoring at a record clip. They beat Louisiana Tech 50 to 0 and Georgia 38 to 6. The Vols scored 34 in a losing effort at Florida, beat LSU at Knoxville 42 to 20, and blasted Duke 52 to 19. The trip to Arkansas allowed the Vols to take revenge on one of the teams that had beaten them in 1982. Arkansas went down 28 to 14.

Heath Shuler and the Vols went to Birmingham for a Saturday afternoon engagement with the Tide on October 16. Alabama was ranked second in the nation and was undefeated with

221

five victories. Tennessee was ranked tenth with the one loss to Florida. A capacity crowd of 83,091 and a regional television audience watched a back and forth game.

Michael Proctor kicked a 22-yard field goal to put Alabama on top on its first drive. Tennessee responded with a 77-yard drive ending with a 25-yard touchdown pass by Shuler to Faulkner. Heath had completed five passes on five attempts in the drive. The touchdown pass gave Shuler nineteen for the season, breaking the record of eighteen set by the Swamp Rat in 1966.

Proctor kicked another field goal in the second to make it Tennessee 7, Alabama 6. Antonio Langham intercepted a Shuler pass a couple of plays later, and Alabama kicked a 30-yard field goal, giving them the lead at 9 to 7. The half ended with that score.

Shuler would not complete another pass the remainder of the game. A hard tackle on the first series of the third quarter gave him a slight left shoulder separation. He continued to play.

DeRon Jenkins pilfered a Jay Barker pass to give the Vols the ball at the Alabama eighteen. The offense couldn't move and settled for a Becksvoort 34-yard field goal. It was Tennessee 10, Alabama 9, entering the fourth quarter.

"The separation was hindering my throwing. I throw with the use of my left arm just as much as I use my right. I couldn't follow through. Alabama didn't know I was hurt. They were giving us the run anyway. The run was there," Heath explained in 1994.

On the first play of the fourth quarter, Charlie Garner, the Tennessee tailback who combined power, speed, and a slashing style, broke through a hole opened by Jason Layman and Kevin Mays and ran for seventy-three joyous—to Vol fans—yards for a touchdown. Tennessee 17, Alabama 9.

Tennessee and Alabama each had three more possessions in the fourth quarter until there was only a minute and forty-four seconds remaining. Tom Hutton punted, and Alabama took it at their 18-yard line, eighty-two-yards from a score. Heath could only

222

watch from the sideline as Jay Barker drove Alabama steadily down field on five straight completed passes. On his sixth completion, he found Kevin Lee who took it to within a half foot of the goal. Barker dived in on the next play. Tennessee 17, Alabama 15.

Alabama's all-round player, David Palmer, took the quarterback position under center for the two-point try.

Shuler still gets upset when he discusses the play by Palmer. "The last play? Forget it. I don't want to talk about that. That was ridiculous. Everyone should have known who was getting the ball. We knew he wasn't going to pass. I'd love to have been out on the defensive side of the ball on that play just to try to stop him."

Heath couldn't go out. And Tennessee couldn't stop Palmer. He scored to tie the game at 17. For Alabama it seemed like a victory. The opposite was true for the Vols.

The cycle had run full circuit from 1965. That year Tennessee felt the 7-7 tie was a moral victory of sorts. This time, it was Alabama's turn to celebrate a tie. Tennessee still had not won since 1985.

Heath ended up with 25 touchdowns for the season. Tennessee recovered and went undefeated the remainder of the regular season but lost to Penn State on New Year's Day. Heath is a "great kid," according to Dewey Warren whose touchdown record was erased by Shuler. "He's an excellent quarterback. He's a big kid, has a gun for an arm, is quick, strong, and has great mobility."

Doug Dickey said, "Heath Shuler is probably the outstanding individual talent of a quarterback that's ever been here. He could make the ball go through the air like Bobby Scott, but he could run more like Charlie Fulton. He is, by far, the most complete individual to play that position at the University of Tennessee."

"He's just a phenomenal player and leader. He can be anything and everything on the professional level that he wants," Phillip Fulmer believes.

Bobby Scott concurs: "I think Heath Shuler is probably the greatest quarterback that ever played at the University of Tennessee."

Heath went back to North Carolina just off the "road to nowhere" and later on to a secluded hunting trip, to decide where his future lay. He had finished as runner-up in the Heisman race, but a childhood dream was always to play football in the NFL.

He decided to follow his dream. Drafted as the first quarterback in the first round, Heath will be throwing the ball for the Washington Redskins and wearing the maroon of his high school once again. Western North Carolina and Volunteer fans will adopt the Redskins as one of their favorite professional teams and watch the Vols' most famous and record breaking quarterback on Sundays instead of Saturdays.

The other advice his mother gave Heath was: "Regardless of how good you think you are, there is always someone out there better. The day may come when you think you are the best, but somewhere, someday, there'll be someone who is just as good as you."

Career Statistics
Heath Shuler

| | RUSHING | | PASSING | | |
	CARRIES	YARDS	ATTEMPTS	COMPLETIONS	TD'S
1991	7	24	4	2	1
1992	105	286	224	130	10
1993	46	73	285	184	25
TOTALS	158	383	513	316	36

Chris Cawood

1993

GAME STATS	Tennessee	Alabama
First downs rushing	11	6
First downs passing	7	14
First downs by penalty	1	2
Total first downs	19	22
Attempts rushing	39	39
Yards gained rushing	253	125
Yards lost rushing	27	67
Net yards rushing	226	58
Passes attempted	26	41
Passes completed	15	22
Passes intercepted	2	1
Net yards passing	180	312
Total yards gained	406	370

Quarterback stats	Shuler	Barker
Passes attempted	26	40
Passes completed	15	22
Passes intercepted	2	1
Net yards passing	180	312
Rushing attempts	11	9
Net yards rushing	36	-21
Total yards	216	291

SEASON RECORDS

TENNESSEE
50	La. Tech	0
38	Georgia	6
41	Florida	34
42	LSU	20
52	Duke	19
28	Arkansas	14
17	Alabama	17
55	S Carolina	3
45	Louisville	10
48	Kentucky	0
62	Vanderbilt	14

CITRUS BOWL
13	Penn State	31

ALABAMA
31	Tulane	17
17	Vandy	6
43	Arkansas	3
56	LA Tech	3
17	S Carolina	6
17	Tennessee	17
19	Ole Miss	14
40	Southern Miss	0
13	LSU	17
36	Miss. St	25
14	Auburn	22

SEC CHAMPIONSHIP
13	Florida	28

GATOR BOWL
24	N Carolina	10

225

Heath Shuler gave his best as a Volunteer and was prepared to do the same for the Redskins.

A Look Ahead

After the 1965 tie, Alabama won the following year's game in Knoxville. Then, Tennessee won four straight.

After the 1993 tie, will Tennessee win or lose in 1994, and what lies ahead? Many readers of this book will know the immediate answer for 1994 before they reach this chapter.

Jerry Colquitt, Todd Helton, Peyton Manning, and Branndon Stewart are four of the ones in line to lead the Volunteers from the quarterback position for this year and some to come. Compared to the quarterbacks of the past, which ones appear to have a better shot at success against Alabama?

Was Heath Shuler correct? Is there too much emphasis on the Alabama game? Yes and no. He was right that every player should be up and ready to play at a hundred per cent regardless of the opponent. Yet, over the last thirty-five years, Alabama has set an example for other teams to follow. If a team beats Alabama, it usually means that team is on the road to success.

The Alabama rivalry began in earnest in 1928 after the Tide had already won more than one National Championship. Except for 1943, Tennessee and Alabama have played on the third Saturday in October of every year. The winner usually has gone on to bigger and better things, while the loser has tried to salvage the season. In order to defeat either Tennessee or Alabama, the opponent has to play good basic football. Defense, the kicking game, blocking, and tackling have to be sound. The quarterback

227

has to lead an offense that is anchored by a talented line and balanced by strong running. When Alabama was losing to Tennessee in 1967-70, the Tide had gotten away from running and relied too much on passing. When Bear Bryant changed to the wishbone he won eight SEC championships.

If history is any indication, a Tennessee quarterback may have done well not to have been born or gone to high school in the state. No quarterback who led his team over Alabama has been a native of the state or gone to high school in Tennessee. That does not bode well for Colquitt or Helton, who both were born in the state and went to high school here.

Colquitt's jersey number has never been worn by a quarterback who led the team to victory over Alabama. Helton's Number 2 has never seen the back of a winning quarterback in the rivalry with Alabama. It could be up to one of them to make his own tradition.

Both of the incoming freshmen quarterbacks have jersey numbers that have significance in the Alabama rivalry. Stewart wears No. 6, which was also Alan Cockrell's number. Cockrell was in on two wins against the Tide. Manning will wear Number 16 which was the Swamp Rat's.

Also, Tennessee's winning quarterbacks against Alabama have always won their first matchup before their senior year, except for Warren who only played as the holder for extra points and field goal attempts in 1967, and Daryl Dickey, who held the team together in the last quarter of the 1985 game.

On the plus side, Colquitt has shown the tenacity, perseverance, and patience to wait his turn when he could have left and played somewhere else. Like the early quarterbacks in this book, Colquit had talent but was behind someone who was doing quite well himself.

Unless he is injured or something unforeseen occurs, Colquitt will get his chance. He will open in September at UCLA and against Georgia at Athens. The position is his to keep or lose, depending upon his handling of it. It's not likely that he would be benched even with a rough outing or two.

If Manning or Stewart are starting by the time Alabama week arrives, it will mean that Tennessee has already lost at least two games. At that point the coaches might then drop back and do what Alan Cockrell's father said when he was going to start as a freshman. "I guess they figured if they were going to lose, they might as well lose with a freshman as a senior."

Coach Phillip Fulmer knows it is more difficult for a freshman to start now than when Cockrell did back in 1981. Both the offensive and defensive schemes are more complex. Manning, having grown up in a home where his father was a great college and professional quarterback, might be able to pull it off sooner than anyone. He also might listen to the advice that Heath Shuler gave himself, which was to sit and watch an experienced quarterback for a year before being thrown into the fray.

The 1994 team will have a strong supporting staff for whichever quarterback ends up playing. That could help to take the pressure off Colquitt, Helton, or one of the freshmen.

Stewart and Manning will, in years to come, be in similar situations as Dewey Warren, Charlie Fulton, and Bubba Wyche. There will be a lot of talent, but only one can play at a time. If they handle it like the triumvirate of 1965-67, it will be to Tennessee's benefit.

Dewey Warren—The Swamp Rat—never played a complete game when Tennessee beat Alabama. The legacy of the Swamp Rat was not that he or any other quarterback single-handedly beat Alabama, but that he did everything necessary to see that Tennessee was successful, even if that was just holding for extra points and a field goal.

George Cafego's advice to the Swamp Rat is just as applicable today as it was in the 1960's: "If you ever get your chance, take advantage of it. Be ready to play when you're called on. Take advantage and do your best."

Those who are willing to do the same will always have a place in Tennessee football lore.

229

Acknowledgments and Errors

A project of this type couldn't have been accomplished without the help and cooperation of many people.

First, let me thank my hardworking editor, Gaynell Seale, who always manages to throw in just the right number of commas, throw out repetitions when they add nothing, and otherwise to keep my writing as grammatical and on course as possible. She has aided me with several projects in the past and continues to be an industrious and skillful helper. A native of Texas, she has come to appreciate the history behind Tennessee football as she worked on this book.

To Jerry Seale, Gaynell's husband, and Sara Cawood, my wife, I express my sincere thanks for allowing me and Gaynell the time to work on this project. Although we worked at separate locations, miles apart, we often talked about the project with the indulgence of our spouses.

Usha Rao designed the cover and brought to life the vision that I wanted for the book.

To all the quarterbacks, coaches, and former coaches who allowed me time to talk with them, I express my gratitude. Perhaps a book could have been written about each one. I found it very difficult to cull through the material and interview quotes I had from them in order to keep the length of the chapters and book down to a manageable size. They are a great group.

Again, I want to thank John Brannon for his interview notes on Tony Robinson. They proved invaluable, along with the photographs of Tony in prison.

Many of the photos used were provided with the assistance of the University of Tennessee sports information department. Bud Ford aided me greatly, and so did Susie Treis. Billy Henry in the athletic department seems to be able to keep up with where everyone is and helped me in finding some of the subjects.

Felice Bryant kindly let me use "Rocky Top" which has become a rousing rallying song for Vol faithful. Thanks also to her able assistant, Sylvia Bennett.

Dr. W. J. Julian, Ray Mears, Lester McClain, and Tim Priest provided interesting information and viewpoints. Boyce Deitz and Frank Maennle, coaches at Swain County High, were very kind in giving of their time and thoughts on Heath Shuler's high school background and recruiting.

For factual background, I relied on interviews, records of the University of Tennessee, and newspaper reports from the Knoxville *Journal* and Knoxville *News-Sentinel*.

The late Ed Harris of the *Journal* had an excellent series of articles in 1964 about Tennessee's football history titled "From T to T at Tennessee." Much factual material was borrowed from that series.

Tom Anderson's articles in the *Journal* also provided me with more details and color.

Ben Byrd, who was sports editor at the *Journal* and a writer for many years before that, wrote some of the best stories on the Tennessee-Alabama series that I found. I owe a debt of gratitude to him for giving me insight through his articles.

The same holds true for some of the great writers at the *News-Sentinel* like Tom Siler and Marvin West. Personally, Marvin West and Ben Byrd were always my favorite sports writers on Tennessee football.

There were many other scribes at both papers who covered Vol football very competently and whose stories I relied upon for factual background. Among those are: Thomas O'Toole, Gordon Smith, Russ Bebb, Victor Lee, Cindy McConkey, Randy Moore, Al

231

Browning, John Adams, Gary Lundy, Ted Riggs, Mike Strange, and Roland Julian.

I always enjoyed the late Bill Dyer's "DyerGrams" of Tennessee football, and I know others did also. Thanks to the Knoxville New-Sentinel Company for allowing the use of them in this book.

Volunteer football fans are a very discerning lot. You can hardly ever get any error or omission by them. I tried very hard for accuracy in this book. However, I realize in a work of this nature, I am bound to have misspelled someone's name, used a wrong statistic here or there, or perhaps named one player when it should have been someone else. I will try to do better. If you find an error, make a note and send it to me: Chris Cawood P.O. Box 124, Kingston, Tennessee 37763. I will do my best to correct it for the next edition of this book. My intent was to be as accurate as I could.

The chapter titled "The Bear Visits the Swamp Rat" is "faction." It is based on facts that did occur. The conversation, setting, and exact date is fictionalized for the purpose of telling the story.

If you have gotten this far, it means you are either a true Vol fan who devours every word written about Tennessee football or you decided to read the last page first in order to see if you might like to read the whole thing. Either way—THANKS.